THE *SECRET OF SECRETS (SECRETA SECRETORUM)*

A Modern Translation, with Introduction,
of *The Governance of Princes*

THE *SECRET OF SECRETS (SECRETA SECRETORUM)*

A Modern Translation, with Introduction,
of *The Governance of Princes*

Lin Kerns

With a Foreword by
Elizabeth Matthew

The Edwin Mellen Press
Lewiston•Queenston•Lampeter

Library of Congress Cataloging-in-Publication Data

Secretum secretorum. English.
 The Secret of secrets (Secreta secretorum) : a modern translation, with introduction, of
The governance of princes / translated and introduced by Linda [Lin] K. Kerns with a
foreword by Elizabeth Matthew.
       p. cm.
 Modern translation of James Yonge's manuscript, the Gouernaunce of prynces.
 Includes bibliographical references.
 ISBN-13: 978-0-7734-5118-6 ((hardcover) : alk. paper)
 ISBN-10: 0-7734-5118-8 ((hardcover) : alk. paper)
 1. Education of princes. I. Kerns, Linda [Lin] K. II. Yonge, James. III. Title.
IV. Title: Governance of princes.
 JC393.A3S413 2008
                              2008013501

hors série.

A CIP catalog record for this book is available from the British Library.

Front cover: Fifteenth-century architectural representation of the Ormond shield at Holycross Abbey
By permission of Roger Stalley, Irish architectural historian

The Edwin Mellen Press
Box 450
Lewiston, New York
USA 14092-0450

The Edwin Mellen Press
Box 67
Queenston, Ontario
CANADA L0S 1L0

The Edwin Mellen Press, Ltd.
Lampeter, Ceredigion, Wales
UNITED KINGDOM SA48 8LT

Printed in the United States of America

This book is dedicated to my father and ever my best friend,

Kermit Harbert

Table of Contents

Foreword

James Yonge's *Governance of Princes* undoubtedly deserves to be more widely known and studied. Though invaluable for specialists, the late nineteenth-century edition by Robert Steele is daunting for those unused to decoding late medieval English prose. This new edition, providing a modern English translation, is most welcome.

Lin Kerns' work in preparing it mirrors the task of the original author in early fifteenth-century Ireland. James Yonge, a Dublin notary commissioned by his patron, James Butler, fourth earl of Ormond, to turn some good book in Latin or French on the art of government into English, the earl's mother tongue, was thus also a translator. He, too, was using his linguistic expertise to make an informative text more accessible to his contemporaries. The text he chose, the pseudo-Aristotelian *Secreta Secretorum*, had a wide currency in late medieval Europe. The insights Yonge's version offers into late medieval political thought are therefore not confined to the particular Anglo-Irish context in which he lived and worked. The very popularity of the *Secreta*, ensuring its survival in other forms—and modern editions—might suggest that there would be relatively little to be gained from rendering this particular translation into modern prose, but readers already familiar with Yonge's *Governance* recognise its unique interest and importance.

Appreciation of this importance in 1898 unfortunately caused Steele to hurry his edition into print with no more than a single sentence in its brief opening 'Note' to alert readers to the linguistic and historical significance of Yonge's work. Fatally postponed, the fuller introduction Steele promised never appeared. Lin Kerns remedies this omission. Her own introductory assessment of the *Governance* and its significance highlights the fact that Yonge did not merely translate his source, but inserted his own illustrative material and comment. This reveals much about himself and his patron, and about the environment that shaped their activities and concerns in early fifteenth-century Ireland.

A number of historians have already employed Yonge's details of events, and drawn on his opinions, to inform studies of politics and society in late medieval Ireland. The *Governance* was crucial to my own study of the fourth Earl of Ormond's political career. It is also of interest to specialists in late medieval literature. To cite just one example, identification of the influence Langland's *Piers Plowman* in Yonge's exempla and rhetoric has formed one strand of the investigations by Kathryn Kerby-Fulton and Steven Justice into the literary interconnections between London and Dublin in this period. These lines of enquiry offer scope for further investigation; others remain to be identified and explored.

Approaching the *Governance* primarily from a linguistic standpoint, Lin Kerns hopes that her modern translation will not only help students to understand Yonge's work, but encourage them to develop the necessary skills to engage further with Middle English scholarship. As the most substantial, precisely dateable, surviving example of late medieval Hiberno-English prose, the original text of the *Governance* has long provided an invaluable resource for linguistic analysis. But she is equally keen to stress its interpretative possibilities. Her further aim in bringing it to the attention of a wider readership is to encourage new multidisciplinary research in Irish studies. When this vision is realised, her new edition will reap its just reward.

Elizabeth Matthew
Department of History
University of Reading

ACKNOWLEDGMENTS

I would like to recognize the following people for all of their invaluable assistance in this project: the Honorable John Butler, and his father, the Lord Dunboyne, for their knowledge of the Butler family history, Dr. Kieran O' Conor, Professor at Galway University, Ann Darracott of the Maidenhead Civic Society of Berkshire, England, the historians and proprietors of Kilkenny Castle in Ireland, Danielle O'Donovan, and Mrs. Clare Brown of Lambeth Palace Library. Also, to Roger Stalley, an Irish architectural historian, I offer my gratitude for permission to use his photograph of the fifteenth century, architectural representation of the Ormond shield at Holycross Abbey, as the cover of this book. Finally, Three people have played a most vital role in the production of this book: Mrs. Patricia Schultz of Edwin Mellen Books whose patience has rivaled that of Job in the production of this book; Dr. Elizabeth Matthew, Professor at the University of Reading, for her prior work on James Butler and whose generous nature provided me with much needed information and support; My mentor and friend, Dr. Joshua S. Phillips, Professor at the University of Memphis, whose guidance, expertise and encouragement have given me the means to make this dream a reality.

Introduction

In 1422, a small section of Ireland surrounding Dublin held some of the last descendants of the Anglo-Norman invaders still loyal to the crown of England. These people, the Anglo-Irish, inhabited this area that by the later fifteenth century, would be known as "The Pale."[i] The English considered their colony more civilized than native, Gaelic Ireland, and they claimed a solid allegiance to the King of England. Legend supported England's king with the tale of the Spanish Milesians' initial invasion. According to the story, a son of an ancient king of Britain was responsible for the initial colonization of Ireland.[ii] But a change had occurred in the descendants of those initial colonists–a new identity had formed with a new sense of nationalism. Indeed, by the fifteenth century, the Anglo-Irish proclaimed a distinctiveness that, although less clear-cut than that of the Irish or the English, nevertheless constituted a strong group identity. Indeed, *The Governance of Princes* is one of the few surviving pieces of prose produced during this time that is not anonymously written (Seymour 135). The fact that James Yonge placed his name upon the finished work displays a sense of pride in, not only his accomplishments, but also in those of his people.

In 1422, James Yonge, an ambitious inhabitant of this English colony, finished his translation of a document entitled *The Governance of Princes* for his patron, the fourth Earl of Ormond, or as he was better known, the White Earl, James Butler. Yonge composed his manuscript by blending his translation of the pseudo-Aristotelian *Secretum Secretorum* with instances of Irish history. For centuries only a few scholars have recognized the importance of this manuscript, but as interest in Irish studies continues to grow, more scholars are starting to scrutinize and re-evaluate documents that have long lain dormant. Yonge's text is particularly compelling because, as Robert Steele has noted, it is "perhaps the only lengthy work known written in the English of the Pale in the fifteenth century, [and] so is important, linguistically and historically."[iii] However, because Yonge's translation was written in Middle English, and an idiosyncratic Middle English at that, the work has remained limited primarily to medievalists. Because *The Governance of Princes* has much to offer scholarship, a modern translation is needed to give a wider multidisciplinary audience access to this document. I have undertaken here a modern translation of *The Governance of Princes* in order to provide that access to this important and fascinating document.

Origin of *The Governance of Princes*

The Governance of Princes has a rather complicated genealogy.[iv] The original Arabic text, which dates from somewhere before 1000 A.D., presents itself falsely as a translation of a treatise from Aristotle to Alexander the Great and contains numerous examples, often in the form of Biblical parables or historical events that illustrate how to be a good ruler (Manzalaoui Intro ix). Authors who have incorporated parts of this document in their own writings include Albertus Magnus, Roger Bacon, and Sir Gilbert Hay. Chaucer lends the document an honorable mention in his Canterbury catalog in "The Canon's Yeoman's Tale," and he uses its physiognomic theories in his development of "The Pardoner's Tale."[v] Over time, readers have used it in a number of ways, from "imbedding... its teachings in lengthier summas and encyclopedias, detaching [its] individual ethical and gnomic teachings to fit specific circumstances, and quarrying in it for illustrative exempla, adapted to suit local conditions" (Manzalaoui Philip of Tripoli 67). Indeed, this description perfectly matches the use for which James Yonge designed his own version.

Although at a later time, some authors molded *The Governance of Princes* to fit a particular ideology, the scholarly focus of the document, itself, is the translation. Two centuries prior to Yonge's translation, the work made its appearance in the dominant language of Western Europe. Around 1230 CE, during a visit to the Bishop of Tripoli in Lebanon, a clerk named Philip discovered the document, for the first time in hundreds of years, in its entirety. At the Bishop's behest, Philip became the first to translate the complete work into Latin (Williams 1). In France, during the latter half of the thirteenth century, a Dominican, Geoffrey of Waterford, and Servais Copale translated the *Secreta Secretorum* into a vernacular (Stanford 13; Manzalaoui Intro xx). Geoffrey, an Irish Dominican who resided in France, was a former resident of Waterford where the Dominicans maintained a library. Among Geoffrey's known works, the translation of the *Secretum Secretorum* is, by far, his most important.[vi] Geoffrey wrote for his patron, as Yonge would for his own more than one hundred years later:

> ... you desire to add a book called the Secrets of Secrets of the most wise philosopher Aristotle, and for this end you have requested me, that I would for your sake translate the said work from Latin into French, which I had already translated from Greek into Arabic, and again from Arabic into Latin... You are further to understand that I have added many other things which, though they are not contained in that book, yet are drawn from other authentic books, and are no less profitable than what is written in that treatise; these things that are added being pertinent to the subject in hand. (Seymour 32)

Geoffrey's claim about his methodology in translating is highly questionable. Geoffrey and Copale seem merely to have translated from Latin into the French (Bliss and Long 735).[vii] However, Geoffrey's admission that he translated with considerable freedom does seem accurate. Yonge would follow in this tradition of taking great license when translating.

In 1420, the newly appointed Lieutenant of Ireland and the fourth earl of Ormond, James Butler, commissioned Yonge, a Dublin notary, to produce an English version of this same treatise in celebration of his appointment (Matthew, 2004, 147). Eager to prove himself as a writer, Yonge accepted. His earlier work probably consisted of a very loose translation of *The English Conquest of Ireland*, originally written by Gerald of Wales.[viii] While we know from his manifest ability with Latin that he could have handled a Latin manuscript for his translation of *The Governance of Princes,* Yonge turned to Geoffrey and Copale's version, which was among the numerous French translations available to him. Taking two years to accomplish the task, Yonge translated this new version of *The Governance of Princes* from French into Middle English. Yonge's manuscript shares central elements with other versions of the *Secreta Secretorum*, one of which is the act of interrupting the flow of exempla in order to insert special commentaries. It is believed that Geoffrey/Copale interpolated the French versions that contained these treatises, the *Liber diaetarum universalium* of Isaac Judaeus and the *Breviloquium de quattuor virtutibus cardinalibus*, as they are known to exist elsewhere in other versions (Manzalaoui Intro ix-xx). Yonge follows his French predecessors by including the basic form of the *Secretum Secretorum*, but he also introduces current events pertaining to Irish history meant to flatter his patron, the fourth earl of Ormond.

Irish History and *The Governance of Princes*

Yonge's document provides an inside glimpse, from a particular perspective, of fifteenth-century Anglo-Irish culture. At the same time, it describes the establishment and influence of the English within Ireland. While Yonge's *The Governance of Princes* expounds James Butler's importance to Ireland and to the English sovereign, even more importantly, it illuminates the development of an Anglo-Irish identity distinct from that of the English and the Gaelic Irish. By including incidents of Norman conquerors dominating the Irish, Yonge imbues his translation with a sense of patriotism, nationalistic energy, and loyalty, not only to his patron, but also to the imbedded Norman Culture left in Ireland.[ix]

Although a dedicated scribe, James Yonge's examples from Irish history in *The Governance of Princes* are not always accurate. He gives full sway to his nationalistic prejudices in examples that support Anglo-Irish supremacy. Yonge's prejudice can be seen in the advice he gives to James Butler regarding the Irish:

> For as a spark of fire raises a huge fire able to burn a realm, so rises from the root of a false enemy, open traitors, other rebels; many wicked weeds soon grow, so that all true men in the land grieve sorely. Therefore, when they fall into your hands, raze them all out by the root, as the good gardener does the nettles (see Ch. 27 GOP).

Yonge compares the Irish to "nettles" several times throughout his manuscript and at every opportunity; he admonishes the "wild Irish" with an emotion akin to loathing. Yonge's insertion of exempla within the traditional parables of the *Secretum Secretorum* is equally emotionally charged.

Yonge uses mythical imagery throughout various points in his document to present the Butlers and the Anglo-Irish in an exalted light. 'Consider Yonge's defense in Chapter 33 of the right of the king of England to lordship in Ireland: "Of the Kynges titles to the land of Irland, aftyr the Cronyclis." Although Yonge refers here to some accurate historical detail from the late twelfth and late fourteenth centuries, he also relates a mythic story of how the first Irishmen came from Bayonne, which was under English control and then how the English king granted those first subjects the property that was proto-Ireland.

Another instance of Yonge's mythical discourse in *The Governance of Princes,* concerns James Butler, the actual second Earl of Ormond (his patron's grandfather) who led one of the most famous battles against the Irish at the Red Moor of Athy. Yonge reports that, during the battle, the sun stood still for a period of three hours until the earl's forces finished decimating the Irish. Yonge also continues to portray the White Earl's exploits against the Irish factions as equally supernaturally supported; "God and oure kynge haue grauntid [Butler] Powere," he claims to do "thereof Execucion in opyn [against] fals enemys, traytouris, and rebelle" (164). This was, of course, a standard literary practice. By exalting the God-given right to dominate another culture, a writer could impose a sense of legitimacy on events. Even more importantly, Yonge's manner of presentation creates a new myth for the Anglo-Irish; the Butlers ride like avenging angels against the wild Irish lords and with their supernatural strength and power, they conquer the land for God and King. Yonge implies that the lineage of James Butler enjoys the approval of God much as did Joshua, the ancient commander of the heavens in the Old Testament. Likewise, Yonge's religious interludes present a narrative structure that fits easily between the legends and fables of historical figures. Yonge's new myth for the Anglo-Irish, his words, stand beside those written by renowned authors of old, and by association gain significance. Even though the evidence of Irish history would dispel Yonge's accounts in most instances, it is Yonge's presentation-- his voice and the importance it confers upon events and the people of his time-- that directs the reader's attention to what was a major concern for the inhabitants of the English colony: the control of Irish interests.

In closely examining Yonge's presentation of two of the fourth earl's exploits, Elizabeth Matthew has provided an interesting perspective on the political state of the English colony, which also helps to illuminate Yonge's compositional practices. In the first instance, she describes Butler's incursion into Thomond, an area "originally granted in 1276 as a lordship by Edward I to

Thomas de Clare, younger brother of the then earl of Gloucester;" by the end of 1420, Butler "had achieved a real extension of royal authority in the west and southwest of Ireland" (Matthew, Diss., 137).[x] In inserting this story, Yonge effectively promotes Anglo-Irish leadership, while ensuring that England will have a permanent reminder of Butler's accomplishments and presumably, Yonge means to raise the Earl's status in the eyes of England's rulers. The second example that Matthew mentions concerns the confinement of Eoghan O'Neill's, an Irish chieftain, by his cousin and rival, O'Neill of Clandeboy. This confinement had prevented Butler from meeting with the former in order to attain peace. In Chapter 43 of *The Governance of Princes*, Yonge relates Butler's retaliation: Butler, through the prayers of the Irish priests, led the "Hoste of Deuelyn (Dublin)" to destroy Butler's enemies so that the conquered were "to Pees reformed" (203). Still, it was an unsteady peace that Butler maintained. The Irish chieftains were constantly in a state of battle with each other, and they did not welcome the English presence in any form. By the end of 1422, Butler's two year lieutenancy had expired and Henry V had died. Yonge's purpose in decorating his work with descriptive examples of specific incidents assured the English government that the Butlers could handle their tumultuous Irish homeland. More importantly, Yonge's enthusiasm and word choice emphasize his belief that the Anglo-Irish were a special breed of men who persevered, wholly under the protection of God, and who were more than capable of keeping the peace.

Although Yonge believed that the Anglo-Irish always enjoyed such divine protection, the real identity of his people was formed from tumultuous political circumstances. Beginning with the reign of Henry II in the mid 12th century, Ireland's relationship to the English Crown was precarious. Until the later fourteenth century, Ireland was expected to be self-sufficient financially and militarily, but the English government in Ireland still had considerable difficulties throughout the reigns of Richard II, Henry IV and his son, Henry V, who was roughly the same age as James Butler.[xi] A. J. Otway-Ruthven claims that "one of the major factors weakening the [Anglo-Irish] colony... was certainly the constant state of warfare among themselves into which certain of the settlers had fallen" (374). However, the Irish warlords, a highly factious lot, were just as quarrelsome among themselves. In a sense, there was a balance of power due to the inner strife in both, the Irish and the Anglo-Irish. But, according to his enemies and to his credit, the White Earl relied on other means to keep control of his part of Ireland. Butler was accused of "packing the Anglo-Irish House of Commons with his own grooms and household servants, even with Irishmen, and inciting Irish chiefs and rebel English to rise in war whenever his political opponents held the supreme office" (Simms 94-95). Although these alleged events would have blatantly defied the Statutes of Kilkenny, which prohibited the Anglo-Irish from consorting with the Irish in any form, Butler's keen appreciation for political action implies that the man's strength in intellect equally matched his physical prowess.

The history of the Statutes of Kilkenny (1366) sheds light on the state of Ireland during the mid-fourteenth to fifteenth century. In the early fourteenth century, extortion ran rampant, as members of the English and Irish aristocracy plundered Dublin. Many colonists attempted to flee, but in 1353, a royal proclamation forbade the departure of "any ecclesiastic, noble, or able-bodied man" from Ireland (Hitchcock 199). Furthermore, it seemed that the English who were born and reared on Irish soil were adopting far too many Irish customs. Many of them had adopted Irish customs and also, taken on Irish names; in short, the Statues of Kilkenny required the denizens of the English colony to speak English, to avoid participating in Irish sports, to not intermarry with the Irish, and to not worship together (Dolan 214). On the other hand, the English barred the Irish by royal edict from holding any type of command, office, or ecclesiastical post. Trade between the two nationalities in time of war became a felony, and regardless of circumstance, the Anglo-Irish were fined for wearing Irish garments or using Irish goods (Hitchcock 201). For the Anglo-Irish, this situation was tantamount to apartheid; "the English government was now converted to the Anglo-Irish commons' view of themselves as a beleaguered outpost of civilization" (Simms 88). However, according to Art Cosgrove, the English settlers, "numerically inferior and lacking a real cultural tradition of their own," inevitably assimilated the surrounding Irish culture" (555).[xii] Therefore, the Anglo-Irish established a culture among themselves that blended aspects of English and Irish societies.

Ironically it was England's prohibitions that pushed the English inhabitants of Ireland to adopt Irish customs. Yonge mentions the Statutes of Kilkenny briefly in Chapter 26, writing of those who would praise a king as false friends, and Yonge states that anyone who is kind to a sycophantic Rhymer, "… brekyth the statutis of kylkeny, and he is acursid by a xj bisschopis, as the same Statutes makyth mencion."[xiii] Yonge clearly wishes to acknowledge English law, but he conveniently ignores those same Statutes regarding to the Anglo-Irish. The institution of the Statutes of Kilkenny strained the relationship between the Anglo-Irish and English, as the Anglo-Irish in form and practice, as Yonge asserts, paid lip service to the law and little else. However, for Butler there was certainly no question of abandoning English allegiance. In 1421 he and the parliament of Ireland urged Henry V to lead an expedition to Ireland. According to Matthew, this request was supported with a carefully researched justification of the legitimacy of royal lordship over both English and Gaelic Ireland similar to the one set out more fully by Yonge in Chapter 33. (Matthew, Diss., 147–51; Matthew, 2004, 148–9). Henry V, whom Butler had accompanied on several of his campaigns, promoted the translation of literature into English and the increasing use of English in government business. While Butler probably never intended to use *The Governance of Princes* to form a comprehensive, unifying language for the Anglo-Irish, the language of the text demonstrates, not only the need to appeal to the King's choice, but perhaps, to emphasize the loyalty of the Anglo-Irish to the crown.

By the end of the 14th century, French was no longer the choice language of Literature and even the use of English was waning, due to the depopulation of Ireland by the English (Seymour 7). According to Terence Dolan, in his essay, "Writing in Ireland," the Statues of Kilkenny was the determining voice for the primary language of both Ireland and England (213-214). But by using English as the language of the text, Yonge affirms Butler's claim that the English in Ireland are granted control of their culture through the sovereign right of the king of England, and, following Butler's lead, he also implies that the Anglo-Irish conforms to this sovereign law.

Yonge implies that the lineage of James Butler enjoys the approval of God much as did Joshua, the ancient commander of the heavens in the Old Testament. Likewise, Yonge's religious interludes present a narrative structure that fits easily between the legends and fables of historical figures. Yonge writes a new myth for Ireland; his words stand beside those written by renowned authors of old, and by association gain significance. Even though the evidence of Irish history would dispel Yonge's accounts in most instances, it is Yonge's presentation-- his voice and the importance it confers upon events and the people of his time-- that directs the reader's attention to what was a major concern for the inhabitants of the English colony: the control of Irish interests.

James Yonge

There is no contemporaneous source of information about the life of James Yonge, but what is known creates a curious picture. Yonge describes himself as "a notary imperial, and the least of the writers and citizens of Dublin".[xiv] Humility aside, there are few recorded instances of James Yonge outside of his written works. He was born of well-established Anglo-Irish parents, who were "closely connected" to the parish of Dublin (Seymour 135).

Although his parents' names are not recorded, Dublin parish records show possible brothers, John and William, during James' lifetime. Yonge's career began in Dublin as a notary, but he, at least once (in 1417), offered his services as an attorney for a "property transaction". Yonge was sent to prison in 1405 for refusing to "sign and seal certain documents" (Seymour 135). In January 1423, he was again imprisoned for nine months, but received a full pardon after being moved to Dublin Castle. Other than the two aforementioned works, The *English Conquest of Ireland* and *The Governance of Princes*, Yonge also wrote an account, in Latin, of a journey, made by Laurentius Ratholdus of Paazthó of Hungary to St. Patrick's Purgatory. As a "notarius imperialis" (clerk in the royal chancery), Yonge probably ended his life with a measure of respect.[xv]

Sections of *The Governance of Princes*

The general influence of the *Secreta Secretorum*—in its many versions—grew in England during the Middle Ages as its accessibility allowed the laity to become familiar with it. In his book, *The Secret of Secrets,* Steven Williams describes many instances in which *The Governance of Princes*, in one of its several translations, was used in college lectures, debates, or in church sermons. However, since Aristotle's other works provided authentic fare for scholars, the *Secreta Secretorum/Governance of Princes* was progressively ignored as its authenticity was increasingly called into question (Williams 258-259). Although considered a "minor work," with over six hundred manuscripts in circulation, the *Secreta Secretorum* was undoubtedly one of the most read, discussed, and absorbed works of the time (349). Obviously, the public did not care who wrote the *Secreta Secretorum*; they flocked to sermons based on the tenets prescribed in the manuscript, especially those views in the sections on physiognomy.

As Yonge's manuscript was especially tailored for the White Earl, his step by step manual for good leadership assumes a more intimate design than other versions. Chapters 1-16 are devoted to the right qualities and behavior that a king should have; chapters 17-44 describe the four cardinal virtues and how a leader should apply himself to them; chapters 45-54 are a loose conglomerate of various topics, such as members of the king's council, as well as advice regarding the inner nature of man. Chapter 55 begins the section on physiognomy, which relates the characteristics of a person to certain physical attributes and Chapters 60-71 contain various methods to ensure good health. Even as Geoffrey omitted the sections on onomancy, so Yonge followed suit. In short, Yonge's text has been reworked for the sake of Christianity, as well as for the Anglo-Irish whose leaders, according to the text, always display the aforementioned qualities for good leadership.

The Two Versions of *The Governance of Princes*

The particular text that I use for my own translation is Robert Steele's transcription of Yonge's original translation of *The Governance of Princes* from the Bodleian Library, Oxford, MS. Rawlinson B. 490. Steele originally included Yonge's version in his *Three Prose Versions of the Secretorum*, 1898.[xvi] Another manuscript, nearly identical in content with the Bodleian, can be found in the Library of Lambeth Palace, MS Carew 596. A signature copy of the same manuscript, which is thought to have been composed late in the 15th century, resides at Trinity College (TCD 592 (T)). Another, incomplete, version of *The Governance of Princes* is also listed in Carew 633, (*Calendar of Carew* MSS; *Book of Howth*, 331-333). This fragment includes only the introduction and the last chapter.[xvii] There is some mystery involved, as Steele refers to the Lambeth

Palace manuscript as MS. 633 in a footnote to indicate where he begins transcribing from this version.

A closer look at the Bodleian and Lambeth Palace original manuscripts reveals some interesting variations. Both texts are written in the Bastard Secretary hand and both display handwriting of several different scribes. Within the Bodleian text, pages are missing from near the end of Chapter 35 (stories of examples of temperance) to the beginning lines of Chapter 39 (on astronomy). Steele fills the gap by referring to the Lambeth Palace manuscript, making sure to point out precisely where he stopped and began again transcribing from the Bodleian version. The Bodleian's superior quality may explain his decision.

The Lambeth Palace version does not regularly separate unrelated items into subset paragraphs. In fact, the table of contents reads as if it were one continuous flow of words. Although both versions use a different color of ink for the Latin quotes, the Lambeth Palace text is very difficult to decipher. The Lambeth Palace version also includes fewer marginal notes than the Bodleian's, and on the whole, the scribes of the Lambeth Palace manuscript made more errors, as witnessed by the corrections found in the bottom margins of the page or inserted above the mistaken lines. Furthermore, in the Bodleian version, the left, right, and bottom margins of the pages contain numerous commentaries, as well as side notes to alert the reader of proximate content.

Literary dialect is also different in the two manuscripts. O. Waterhouse in *Early English Text Society*, (Ex. Ser. No. 104, pp. xlvii and lxvii) describes the attributes of fifteenth century Dublin manuscripts:

> The confusion of *th* with *t* and *d*.
> The confusion of *w* with *u* and *v*.
> The omission and erroneous insertion of *h*.
> Substitution of *t* for final *d*.

Substitution of *sh* for *s*.

Substitution of *ss* for *sh*. (Seymour 11)[xviii]

The first three characteristics can be found in both manuscripts; however, the final two are found only in the Lambeth Palace text. Also, a scribe uses *i* for *y* in many instances, as well as the superfluous use of double consonants. For example, in the Bodleian version, *called* is *callid*; in the Lambeth Palace manuscript, the same word is represented by *callitte*. The Lambeth Palace document also omits certain articles, such as *the*, and certain words lose their final consonants. A common example is that the Bodleian's "aftyr" is spelled as "aft" in the Lambeth Palace version. Spelling, in general, is much more variable in the Lambeth version than in the Bodleian. Assuming that Steele also noticed these differences, it is small wonder that he chose the Bodleian manuscript for his parent source.

Perhaps the most interesting difference between the two manuscripts is seen in the final benediction by the author(s). The Bodleian text ends Chapter 71 with:

> Fro al manere of myschefe, almyghty god de-fende oure lyge lorde, kynge henry the Fyfte, and James the Botillere, Erle of Ormond, his lyeutenaunt of Irlande, Whyche this boke to translate me comaundet, And graunt ham, grete god, and al hare Subiectis, in the Sewyn Vertues, grace al tymes to growe. Amen. Laus deo clementissimo.I-thankyd be god, that is so Hende, That of this Worke hath maket an ende.

Compare the Bodleian text with the following concluding statement from the Lambeth Palace version:

> And fro all manner of mychef all mighty God defend now vs, and all that ben alyue in gode in godes vertuis; and all that ben in ille

lif all mighty God send tham grace that they mow be amendit into a better lif. Amen. "Explicit, with moch a doo. I prey God neuer sorrow my hart cum to. [xix]

There is no explanation as to why the endings vary, nor is there a reason why at the end of the Lambeth Palace version, a few pages are filled with a sketch of a squire, which flanks repeated scribbling variations of the same couplet ("ffarewell adue I must nedes thee hend / My labour is lost, I gett no pens"), and several efforts to improve the appearance of a particular blocked letter. Regardless of their origin, the presence of such intimate scribblings from the hand that placed quill to parchment adds an extra touch of humanity to the text that preceded it.

The Translation

In translating Yonge's version of *The Governance of Princes* I have tried to approach the text with seriousness and scrupulous attention. With any task involving translating, the demon to exorcise is the one that tempts the translator to overly insert herself into the text. In order to retain the flavor and spirit of Yonge's time and his pedantic tone, the nomenclature he uses and the contemporary terminology have been retained as much as possible. I have tried to make this translation as literal and as accurate as I could. I have also made every effort to verify dates and names; and modern spellings supersede those of the Middle Ages. However, this translation's commentary makes no claim to be the final word on the many subjects that *The Governance of Princes* involve and invoke. The sections where Yonge describes his vision of Irish events, as they relate to the topic at hand, is hopefully the beginning of much lively discussion. My purpose here is not as a scholar of Irish history, but as a translator who hopes to open the discussion on a fascinating topic.

Secondly, I have occasionally rearranged syntax and punctuation. The original is teeming with run-on sentences, non-according subjects and verbs, dangling participles, and rampant punctuation marks situated seemingly at random. I have tried to use punctuation as a way to remain consistent with the meaning of the original text and also to provide emphasis where needed.

Third, the only words that have been omitted from *The Governance of Princes* are the superfluous prepositions that bear no meaning to the whole; indeed, the copious use of "of" becomes distracting and bothersome after one encounters it repeatedly. Middle English words often have several distinct meanings. In translating, I have privileged the semantic rather than the lexical unit. In other words, I have chosen to use whatever word, or words, most closely approximates the sense of the original. In doing so, I have lost some of the lexical repetition that Yonge favored. Also, in addition to references cited, I have added a list of books designed for further reading on topics related to the subject at hand.

Fourth, Latin used in *The Governance of Princes* has been left as it was originally written, which was generally in bold print. Yonge, in his attempt to persuade readers to use English as the preferred language of scholars, writes his axioms, saws, and prestigious quotes in Latin and then translates them into the vernacular. However, Yonge does not translate original Latin quotes or Christian terminology in his text; he uses the original instead to add reinforcement and authenticity to his translation. My own translation leaves Yonge's methodology intact so that it is presented with the same manner of support, precisely to retain the sense and semblance of the original document. In the past, Manzalaoui has suggested that it would be useful to designate which sections of the original *Sirr al-asrar* correspond to the translated text; truly, this is a project worthy of future scholars who are adept at crossing several language boundaries within the same text.

The intent of this translation has been to capture the quintessence of what I feel to be one of the most important documents of the 15th century Anglo-Irish. In it we hear the voices both of tradition and of a new inquiring spirit. Williams asserts that the "tradition of doubt that had begun in the thirteenth century... triumphed;" this questioning of authenticity opened the path to the scientific method and the infinite path to truth (343). Indeed, the fact that Geoffrey and Copale's version, as well as Yonge's, does not include the accretionary sections on onomancy and alchemy and the lapidary, so common in other versions, are to the work's benefit. Our attention instead is focused upon the literature within Yonge's translation. Regardless of the fact that *The Governance of Princes* was never meant for the mass of society, this text plays an important role in English and Irish history and the attention the English colony receives is invaluable. We come nearer to understanding the formation of a new identity, the Anglo-Irish, and by doing so, we understand more about ourselves. Yonge's masterpiece provides a fascinating and opinionated account of this period in medieval Ireland—one that underscores and portrays the indigenous culture of the Anglo-Irish. In my view, the true literary and historical worth of *The Governance of Princes* can be found in Yonge's depiction of an attitude of belonging, ownership, and superiority of the Anglo-Irish.

It is my hope that many disciplines will benefit from this translation, that art, anthropology, history, and language studies can reap the potential knowledge Yonge's work offers. It is also my hope that further research will be accomplished in Irish studies and that, perhaps, once more the *Secreta Secretorum*, also known as *The Governance of Princes*, will receive the attention it once enjoyed and has always deserved.

Lin Kerns

Notes

---

[i]   Later in the 15th century, English control would shrink to the counties of Louth, Meath, Dublin, and Kildare. It was during this time that an earthen berm was constructed around the area, hence the term, the Pale. Half of Kildare and Meath counties were left out of this encircling rampart (Simms 92).

[ii]   See Chapter 33, *GOP*.

[iii]   Robert Steele's comment appears in a note on an unnumbered page prefacing his text..

[iv]   According to Arabists, this document was originally known as *the Kitab ilm al-siyasa fi tadbir aal-riyasa* (*The Book of the Science of Government on the Good Ordering of Statecraft*), it was commonly known by its shortened name, the *Sirr al-asrar* or the *Secret of Secrets* (Williams 29).

[v]   Lines 1443-1447 read: But if that he th' entencion and speche / Of philosophres understonde kan; / And if he do, he is a lewed man. / For this science and this konnying,"quod he, / "Is of the secree of secrees, pardee" (The Riverside Chaucer 281). For further reading on Chaucer and his connection to the Secreta Secretorum, see the Walter Clyde Curry Papers, MSS. 097, Special Collections, Jean and Alexander Heard Library, Vanderbilt University.

[vi]   Geoffrey's other works include a translation of Dares Phrygius on the Trojan Wars and a translation of Roman history originally written by Eutropius (Seymour 31).

[vii] See also Ed. A. Cosgrove. *A New History of Ireland II: Medieval Ireland, 1169-1534.*

[viii]   Scholars have noted that although Yonge probably did produce the transcription of *The English Invasion of Ireland*, the styles of this text and *The Governance of Princes* do not much resemble each other. However, St. John D. Seymour notes the similarities of dialect within both; words, such as "dure (door), haryme (harm), ather (either), and ayse (ease) are used within both manuscripts (141). Arguments for Yonge as the translator rest on the fact that *The English Invasion of Ireland* is paired with his *Governance of Princes* in the Bodleian archives. Also, regardless of later publications stating that Yonge had no Waterford connections, I am inclined to agree with the editors of The Romantic Review, who state that Yonge probably wrote his version at the city of Waterford. Yonge's use of particular word forms denotes a direct connection with Waterford. Yonge would later produce a work in Latin describing the visit of a Hungarian nobleman, Laurence Rathold, to St. Patrick's Purgatory in order to do penance.

[ix]   According to Elizabeth Matthew in her dissertation "The Governing of the Lancastrian Lordship of Ireland in the time of James Butler, Fourth Earl of Ormond, c. 1420-1452," (University of Durham, 1994). Yonge took care "to embellish the work with illustrative examples of specific incidents and problems in the government of the lordship [which] leaves little room to doubt the earl's pride in the appropriateness of the enterprise [for] his own present task" It is Matthew's belief that Ormond may have been prompted by a desire to impress Henry V with his seriousness of purpose during the king's reign (120).

[x]   In her dissertation, Matthew points out that when the fourth earl campaigned in Thomond is not clear, but that the campaign must have taken place between 1420-1422 (137).

[xi]   Born in 1390, Butler was only three or four years younger than Henry V. For the young Henry's early visit to Ireland with Richard II in 1399, Butler's service to the king outside Ireland before 1420, and the Butler family's later contribution of memories of Henry V to an early sixteenth-century English account of the king's life, see Kingsford (xvi-xxxviii); Wylie and Waugh (445-448); Allmand (12-14); Matthew, Diss. (112-115)'Matthew, 2004 (147).

[xii]   See also Ed. A. Cosgrove. *A New History of Ireland II: Medieval Ireland, 1169-1534.*

[xiii] The Statutes of Kilkenny (1366) had pronounced, "... it is agreed and forbidden that any Irish minstrels, that is to say tympanours, poets, story-tellers, babblers, rymours, harpers or any

other Irish minstrels shall come amongst the English; and that no English shall receive them or make gift to them...": Curtis and McDowell (55); see also Otway-Ruthven, (292).

[xiv] Seymour (135).

[xv] All quotes within this paragraph are taken from Dolan, 2004 (811).

[xvi] Steel published his edition through the Early English Text Society in London, Kegan Paul, Trench, Trübner & Company.

[xvii] Seymour states that Carew mistakenly ascribes the text to a John Yonge instead of James and that the notation was written in Carew's own handwriting (140).

[xviii] Seymour describes this dialect as "early form of English derived from the western and south-western counties of England, from which Dublin, the towns, and large parts of the colony were generally populated" (11).

[xix] According to Carew, the hand changes with "Explicit" and continues until the end (333).

(James Yonge's original preface/dedication to James Butler)

In honor of the High Trinity, Father, Son, and Holy Ghost, Almighty God, our lady, St. Mary, and all the holy saints of heaven, you, noble and gracious lord, James Butler, Earl of Ormond and lieutenant of our liege lord, King Henry V in Ireland, humbly recommends me, your poor servant, James Yonge, to your high lordship. I implore the aforesaid trinity that your honor and profit of body and soul ever increase, all the time desiring this in Christ and with all my heart. Amen. Amen.

The most wise scholars and masters of renown that have been before us in all times, agreed in one teaching, showed one truth, and discussed the prowess and worthiness of emperors, kings, and all the other governors of chivalry: that chivalry is not only kept, saved, and maintained by deeds with arms, but it is kept by wisdom, the help of laws and by knowledge and wisdom in understanding. Without strength and power, this surely does not guide him, but with strength and power he combines wisdom and knowledge, and knowledge directs power. The prince may act in goodness and walk surely with good men. This appears in many old stories, for the understanding and great knowledge of Aristotle would have little helped King Alexander, without the strength of the fame of his power. The old Princes of Rome conquered more of the entire world by knowledge and study of scholarly books than by the assaults of battle or the strength of people. Therefore, Cicero, the great scholar says, "Then, when kings were philosophers and philosophy reigned, there were well governed empires and kingdoms."[1] This same thing is perceived by the skill of your knowledge and the clearness of your intelligence, my noble and gracious, aforementioned lord, and therefore I was enjoined to translate this same good book of *The Governance of Princes* out of Latin and French into your mother tongue, English. Also, much as I am ever bound by your gracious, kindly gentleness to obey your commandment, here now I translate for your sovereign nobleness, the book of Aristotle, Prince of Philosophers, *The Governance of Princes*. This same book in Latin is called *Secreta Secretorum*, that is to say, *The Secret of Secrets*, and it is the same book Aristotle wrote to his disciple, Alexander the Great, emperor and conqueror of the entire world. This Aristotle was Alexander's darling and well beloved scholar, and therefore he made him master and chief counselor of his realm. Therefore many men held him to be a prophet, for Aristotle was a man of great counsel, of profound letters, and perceptive in understanding. Knowing the laws well, he was of a high nature, well proved and learned of all sciences, wise, clever, humble, and always loving right and truth. As I find written in the old books of the Greeks, God sent his angel to him, saying, "Rather I should call you an angel than a man."

Aristotle sent many epistles that man now call letters, to Alexander for the governance of kings and princes and this present book is one. The reason that Aristotle made this epistle was this: when Alexander had conquered Persia, some of the people there were disobedient and against him. He then sent this letter in this form to Aristotle:

"To Aristotle, a noble master of right governance and truth, Alexander, his disciple, sends greetings. By your discretion, I understand that I have found in the land of Persia a people full of reason, high understanding and intelligence, and that before all others, convey dignity in lordship; therefore, we intend to destroy them all. Write to us by letters what you think upon this matter."[2]

On this matter, Aristotle answered in this manner:

"If you may change the air and the waters of that land, and over that the ordinance of the cities, fulfill your purpose, and if not, then govern them with good will and kindness. For if you do so, you may have hope that with God's help, all will be obedient to you, and you will govern them in good peace."

When Alexander had received this letter, he obeyed Aristotle's counsel. Therefore the Persians were more obedient to Alexander than any other people had been. And for as much, noble lord, that I desire more the utterance of your praise, I write this book to your Excellency, that is intermingled with many good examples of old stories, the four cardinal virtues, and diverse other good matters with old and new examples.

4

Here begins the chapters and the titles of this book:

Chapter 1: First, how and for what reason this book of Aristotle's was made

Chapter 2: Two principal things that every king must have

Chapter 3: Examples of old stories to prove the aforesaid lesson true

Chapter 4: Diverse manners of kings that are praised and not praised

Chapter 5: Reasons to shun foolish munificence and greed and what befits

generosity

Chapter 6: What subtlety in understanding and knowledge helps and how they are

known

Chapter 7: Of the two things that cause a king to have a good renown

Chapter 8: How a king should be towards his people

Chapter 9: How a king should be regarding virtues and clothing

Chapter 10: The custom of Jews and how a king should maintain his subjects and

namely his merchandise

Chapter 11: Of the solace of a king

Chapter 12: A king is likened to rain, wind, winter, and summer

Chapter 13: Of the prudence of a king

Chapter 14: Of the mercy of a king

6

8

Expliciunt capitula sequentis libri:

Chapter 1: First, how and for what reason this book of Aristotle's was made:

As far as the reason why this book was made, you will understand that after Alexander had conquered all the lands of Persia and Media, he passed with his retinue towards the land of India to conquer it and that Aristotle was then abiding at school in Greece. Alexander had great need of Aristotle's wise counsel, and because Alexander loved Aristotle so much, Alexander sent for Aristotle via a letter to come to his presence. Aristotle wrote, in good manner to Alexander, the reason why he would not leave the school, in this manner: "O you fully glorious son, fully rightful emperor, confirmed by God in holy truth and with virtue, withdraw from yourself all bestial appetites and your talent will fall to the service and honor of God. Your letter I have received with due reverence and honor, and with full understanding of the desire you have for my presence, but since I can not come now, I send this letter from which you may counsel yourself as if I were with you, so that the highness of your intelligence may, in an easy manner, perceive the depths of subtlety, a little remembrance of knowledge, and that the many ways of truth may be your guide."[3]

Chapter 2: Two principal things that every king must have

Whoever would peaceably maintain lordship and a realm to govern aright, he must have two things. One is that he must be wise, subtle, and remember that after good laws and being wisely righteous, before all things he must judge evenly between all manners of folks, between large and small men and the rich and the powerful, without going outside of the law. The other is the force of power, whereby he may keep, maintain, and defend his realm. This he may accomplish by the first in an easy manner. For whosoever by knowledge and understanding does right to every man, as well as friends, he should be lord of every man, and as a rightful lord, be feared. Such a prince, all men gladly obey. This obedience and force is not only by righteousness, but also by freedom and generosity. Therefore a prince must spend freely among his folk and wisely reward every man, as he deserves, but the mischief that follows chicanery and foolish munificence, you will see it afterwards in this book[4].

Chapter 3: Examples of old stories to prove the aforesaid lesson true

The wise scholar, Valerius, tells about old times when there was a wonderful strictness of rightness in kings to keep the laws well and that king Zaleucus established many good laws in his city of Locris.[5] This was one of them: "That whosoever was guilty of adultery, he should lose both his eyes." Afterwards, it befell that his own son was found guilty of the same sin. The entire city honored and revered the father and desired that he release his son from the pain of his eyes, but by his will, the king would not allow it. Those of the city prayed so entirely and implored the king that he granted that one of his son's eyes be saved. However, because he would not break his law, first he made his own eye to be cut out and saved one of his sons, so he maintained his law and released the duress of the law. So that wonderful evening, he divided himself between the pity of the father and the righteousness of the good and rightful judge of all others. He appeared well by this as, by law, he judged all others rightfully and would not even spare his son. Also, force of power becomes visible, and it is to be known that force of power is not according to the number of people, but according to the might of them that are proud in arms and according to the governance of the knowledgeable and wise prince. For without those numbers of people, little is worth anything to the prince. We find this written that Xerxes, King of India, would battle with the people of Greece; he strongly gathered huge hosts of which no man could tell the number. Wherefore some of his men said that the Greeks would not continue to abide by the tidings of battle, but flee at the first deployment of it. Others said thatthat the Grecians (or Greeks, which you prefer best, in English) would not be discomfited. Therefore because so few people would not join in battle, they would soon all fall down and assume horror at so great a host. Some of his other men said that they feared that they would find the city of Greece empty and that their king would not engage in war so that he could battle or show his power. Others said that the Greeks would scarcely be sufficient to their king's host, not in the enormity of all Greece in land or her sea, for Xerxes had so huge of a retinue that the Greek sea was straight to them. The abundance of his knights was so great that all the level ground of the land would not be enough for their tents and pavilions to be pitched, much less to fight or to make any assault, or that the air might not receive the abundance of their arrows and darts. They flattered the king so much in such a manner that by the force of pride from his host, this flattery made him overturn the wise counsel of Demaratus[6], the proud wise scholar, that said to him, "You should fear greatly, the flattery of the destroyers that please you, for truthfully it is that nothing is too much that it may be governed aright, and that thing that a man may not govern, it may not last. Nothing earthly is so great that it will not perish and fail." And afterwards, it befell what all that his good scholar Demaratus had said betiding the king. For that great host, by a defect in right prudence and wise governance, was overcome and vanquished by few people governed in an orderly manner. However, victory in battle is principally through God. This shows well the deeds of the noble victorious earl, Sir James, your grandsire, who hated lechery in his entire lifetime. Therefore God in all His time granted him marvelous victories upon his enemies with few people, namely upon the Murphys, of whom he slew large amounts of people in the red moors of Athy, a little before the sundown, the sun standing marvelously still till the slaying was done.[7] And since at Astoffy, as Sir Edwards Perrers the good knight can tell, your same grandsire with few people defeated Arthur MacMurrough, discomfited many people, and killed many hundreds of his men.[8] It appears in this example that freedom helps governance. It befell King Alexander one time that one of his knights of his service asked him for a reward. He that was full of freedom and would hire needy men gladly and would more gladly advance them gave his knight a rich and great city. Then said the knight, "Lord, so great a gift does not belong to my poor estate." Alexander answered him, "I promise not what belongs to you to receive, but what suits me to give." All men gladly served King Alexander for that freedom and for many others.

Chapter 4: Diverse manners of kings that are praised and not praised

Kings are demeaned in four manners: some are so by being freehanded to themselves and to their subjects, others are so by being greedy to themselves and to their subjects. Of these two, the Italians say that a king is not to be reproved if he is miserly with himself and free-handed to his subjects, but the Persians say the contrary, that a king is not worthy unless he be free-handed to himself and to his subjects. But among all others, he is the worst and most reproachable who is freehanded and liberal to himself and miserly and hard to his subjects, for his realm may not last. Regarding the aforesaid things, it is appropriate to know what generosity is.[9] Generosity in English is called freeness or freedom. It is necessary to know how it may be had, conquered, and maintained. Also, it is necessary to know what harm foolish munificence and greed cause. Therefore it is necessary to know that it is hard to know how in all points to hold the mean and is it easy to fail, as it is hard to hold the mark, and it is easy to fail. Therefore it is more masterful to know and conquer the generosity that holds the average way, than foolish munificence or avarice that are the two bounds. Therefore if you will live lavishly by the virtue of generosity, you must see to three things. The first is how much you may spend of your own private property. The second is to take heed of what time has given to be the most needful or lacking. The third is that you are advised to see the services and merits of your subjects.

You will understand that if you spend freely of your power that you may give of your own, but if you spend or give away other men's goods, you surpass generosity, and you walk away from freedom. Whoever spends more than his power or his goods stretches and he decreases most in power. Again, that is the virtue of munificence and when this rule is surpassed, whoever follows him must maintain excessive costs for his power without need.[10] He is a waster of his goods; he destroys his realm what he may, as he is not worthy to be a governor. Such a person is called foolishly munificent, or a waster, and he pretends to have wisdom and prudence.[11] Be well advised of the second thing, for if you govern wisely and spend your goods after your power, then namely will you use your munificence to give to your good people when you see them needful and poor. Then you will give yourself and your subjects both, you will find friends without fail with obedience in all things, and your realm will last and grow in force of power and richness. Men in old times praised such a king; such a king is called virtuous, generous, and a good prince. Think cleverly and wisely about the third thing so that you can perceive of the services and of the good deeds for the diversity of your people that have been good, profitable, and true to you. And to them give their rightful desert and to those that are needful, reward well, for whosoever gives to him that needs nothing and deserves nothing, that gift is lost and it is not due to generosity and virtue. It is a foolish and unseemly thing to a king to be stingy and greedy, for none may love such a man and without love, a man may never duly and truly serve. Therefore if any king feels that he is greedy or foolish with munificence, he would do well to ordain some true men that may wisely dispense and ordain those goods that belong to a king.

Chapter 5: Reasons to shun foolish munificence and greed and what befits generosity

Alexander, I say to you to know certainly that a king that gives more than his realm may sustain will soon be destroyed, he will be brought to nothing but his realm will fail most. Whosoever is hard and does not give will not hold a realm. Therefore, know this well that in order to maintain a realm, the king's honor and glory is to shun foolish munificence *and* greed as two wicked enemies.[12] Generosity and great wealth cause a realm to long endure and to be kept well. One thing I shall say that may help you much and that is that you would not take gladly the goods of your subjects nor their possessions. Therefore Hermogenes, the very wise philosopher, says it is a sovereign goodness and a surety of knowledge and of law with a demonstration of perfect virtue in a king if he shuns taking and holding his subjects' goods and their possessions, for that destroys realms.[13] Wherefore, even though this is done so, the king's rule may not last long. Therefore the prophet says, "Unrightful men shall not live half their days" and that also, unrighteousness disinherits kings and princes. Therefore Solomon says, "Kingdoms are transferred from one people into another because of unrighteousness."[14] And therefore the prophet forbids wrongs and says, "You should not covet gluttony or wrongful taking." [15] The gloss thereupon says, "O you damnable lechers with your winnings that gain money and lose conscience." Many princes and lords, for a need, take the goods of the common people, much against their wills, to defend them from mischief. Such a king is tolerable, as many men think, in order to more shun mischief. However, there are some princes that for their own singular advantage, as they believe by the pretence of their prince-hood and the pretended defense of the common people, take true men's goods at their own inclination. Such princes are worse than Satan unless they make amends. Now God in his endless goodness ever grant you the grace to shun extortion and false greed, and be ever well aware that I have no pride in your good deeds, for then you should lessen the reward of God, for from every good deed, two good things will fall out. One is God's reward to the doer of the deed; the other is glory and worship of God. As scholars say, he that prides himself for vaunts of his good deeds deprives the glories and the worship of God and therefore he will lessen the reward that he should receive from God. Pride is one of the most perilous sins there is, for it comes ever from good deeds, and many a man that lives holily perishes having pride for his good living and good deeds. Therefore think entirely and live fully that all goodness is, was, and ever shall be in God, through God, and of God. And thus it lies in no man's power to do well except only by the special grace of God's sufferance.[16] As Christ in the gospel of goodness speaks, says, "**Sine me nichil potestis facere**" ("Without me you may do nothing"). In another place, he says, "**Qui perseuerauerit vsque in finem, hic Saluus erit**" ("Whosoever continues into the end, he shall be saved"). Therefore, gracious lord, the good gracious governance that you have begun, continue, as you desire to save your honesty and all true people of your liege specially will pray for you if you so do. Set in your banner God's blessing and theirs, against which your enemies will have no power to withstand.

Example to prove this true

In King Richard's and King Henry the IV's time, this worshipful knight, Sir Stephen Scrope, having the governance of Ireland, did much extortion, took liberally, and paid little good.[17] He worked much, despoiled little in the Irish, but in the meantime, he had enemies. At last, the excellent lord, Thomas of Lancaster, our liege lord's brother that is now lieutenant of Ireland, made Stephen his deputy and Ireland his to govern. When he was made deputy, he wanted to bring the noble lady, his wife, into the land, but she made a vow to Christ: unless he would swear on a book that he would pay all true men for their own expenses and do no extortion, she would never go into Ireland in his company; that oath he swore. He went into the land and he made good payment to all men. He granted great grace to all the gentry within his power that was allied with the king for life and lands. Therefore, he had blessings of true men in his banner. The power of these armies was so much that in one day he burned the great, proud Arthur MacMurrough's country, in your presence, then tender of age, and killed many of MacMurrough's men. He won the town of Callan in Ossory, and surrendered Walter Burke, a rebel, to the king. He restored O'Carroll in the same town with a huge number of enemies therein, and outside he slew the same Walter, discomfiting them with a great Irish army, all in one day in your aforesaid presence.[18] There was good peace in Leinster that year and he accomplished many other commendable deeds with armies elsewhere. All this grace befell him that year, as I understand, because all that year he did no extortion.

Now I leave this matter and I will write about the book that I had been discussing. It says that extortion taken by a king from his subjects' goods destroys the realm, and it shows that to be true in this manner: when the troubles and the expenses of foolish munificence surpasses the rents, revenues of the realm, and the receipts, then the king takes most of his people's goods. Then he does harm on every side: harm to them from whom he takes, for he bereaves them of their living and their sustenance; extortion and taking harms him that ravishes and takes, for he is undone by falseness. He cries to God almighty, father of mercy and of pity, and God hears him well and blessedly, and such an extortioner He destroys in many ways. His realms are lost by war, by the default of his heirs, by the death of father and son, or by other evil mishaps. It is fitting of generosity in a king that he should not be inquisitive of the riches of other men, neither of their private stores, nor should he remember his gifts. But when a man gives him something, thereupon should he think well. Regarding the virtue of generosity and bounty in a king, it is fitting that he reward those men who did him well in the service of their ancestors, or in their own, though they are old men and may not be able to bear arms, insofar as for a long time before, they have well deserved in battle and in many wars proved themselves in their great youth. Though they have not might and strength to bear arms in their oldness, they have proven their virtue and strength of counsel. One may give a strong stroke in battle and another may give a wise counsel and save all of a realm, where the singular strength of one man cannot do this. It appertains easily to a virtuous king to release the wrong that is done to him, to honor those that are honorable, to help needy men, to counsel those that are unwise, to succor and defend those that are guiltless, to answer gladly the people, and to speak kindly to them, to speak wisely and little, and to flee foolish and evil company. These manners of things a man may not do without wisdom, understanding, and the light of knowledge.

Chapter 6: What subtlety in understanding and in knowledge helps and how they are known[19]

Understand Alexander that knowledge and understanding are the head and the beginning of all governance, the soul's health, the keeping of virtues, and they destroy vices. By the knowledge and wisdom of understanding, a man may well choose the good and leave and shun the evil. Understanding is the beginning and the will of all virtues and the root of all goodness. The desire and willingness for good renown is a sign and a token of knowledge and understanding, and whosoever truly desires good renown shall be renowned and praised. And he that does not desire it shall be undone in the end. Therefore good renown is to be desired by a sovereign, for the governance of a realm is not done at will except through good renown.

Whosoever desires a realm or purchases a lordship or is well without the love of good renown, then he begins with pride and that is the beginning of all wickedness. For pride engenders envy, envy engenders falsehood, and falsehood engenders lying. Lying engenders detraction, detraction engenders hatred, hatred engenders wrong and wrath, and wrong and wrath engender irreverence. Irreverence engenders enmity, enmity engenders discord and war, and war destroys laws and the realm, and that is against reason and nature. Therefore desire good renown, for you may conquer humility that destroys pride. Humility engenders love that destroys envy and hatred; love engenders truth that destroys falsehood, lying, and detraction. Truth engenders rightfulness that destroys wrong, anger, and irreverence. Rightfulness engenders friendship and destroys enmity; friendship engenders counsel, help, and peace. The entire world was

ordained after these virtues and the laws are established in the people, according
to reason and to nature.

Chapter 7: Of the two things that cause a king to have good renown, as it follows in this next chapter.

In so much as a king should foremost desire good renown in foreign
governance and succeed in all that he must do and maintain two things. First and
above all things, he must be subject and obedient to the law of God and all his
realm, and after that he must govern and sustain himself after that law, for only
such a prince is worthy to have lordship. He that makes God's law subject to his
realm and overly subordinates it and mars what he may, and diminishes his
generosity and statutes, by that, he does great villainy before God. He exceeds all
manner of law, right, and truth. He hates God, and in contempt forgets what is
right, such that all of God's people hold in little honor. The philosophers say that
the proper thing for the majesty of a king is that he be subject and obedient to the
stableness of good laws, and above all things, to God's law, not in false hypocrisy
in word or in deed, but by showing and openly working good works, so that all
folks may perceive that he fears God and that he is subject to His might. Then
verily his people shall fear him when they know that he fears God and duly honor
him. However, when a king shows only in word that he fears God and in his
works does the contrary, he shall be cut off from God and his people shall despise
him. Evil works may not be hidden from the people for because of them he will
most lose his people's love, his realm shall fall, and he must fail the crown of his
honor and his reverence.[20] Thereafter, no one will gather possessions or heaps of
treasure that may make his realm return or win his lordship again if he has lost it.
This was proved to be true in King Richard the Second, our former king that I
knew well. This king wedded the worthy Anne of Germany, the emperor's
daughter. Not long thereafter he had the peace of all Christian realms and among
all kings he stood highest in prosperity. When Christ took Anne, he wedded

Elizabeth of France, called the king's daughter, then age nine. Then adultery and lechery reigned in him and his household, so that then the entire realm told rumors about and loathed that abominable sin, the boldness of this marriage, his high alliance, and his baronage. He made Thomas of Woodstock, his own precious uncle, to be a murdered at Calise, and Richard treated the rich, ruly Earl of Arundale evilly by beheading him at Tower Hill, London. He also ill-treated many other noble lords in whom his honor stood. All this he did in anger because this noble lord ruled him for the best in his tender age. While he reigned in this misrule, three years past and he arrived at the land of Ireland and had little or no success. In the meantime, Duke Henry of Lancaster, who Richard had exiled, arrived in east England. Then lords and commoners of the land at Pomfrey came to his help, gathering to him many thousands on every side. Duke Henry went to Westchester; King Richard arrived from Ireland into Wales; there soon scattered all his rich retinue, and at the Castle of Flint, the Duke took him. He led him to London where Parliament was set and the Duke was crowned king. However, after that, Richard could never regain his kingdom, although many thousands of men lost their lives to him. Therefore, by this example and many more, a man may see that unless that a king or any other governor of a people fear God, love Him, and maintain His law before all things, he shall fade, fall, and forgo honor in a short time. The second thing that causes a king to have good renown is that, in speaking, he govern his tongue wisely and that he be not of many words unless he be well advised, reasonably to speak only that which he will do, to consider discretely and subtlety, and to effect his purpose to say and do. Over that, it is necessary that his deeds and his works accord to his words so that he is not variant and unstable. Stability is required of every good prince to have so that a man may know where he can be found. If these two aforesaid things are well maintained in a king, he will have the grace of God, and he will be worshipped, praised and feared by his people.

Chapter 8: How a king should be towards his people[21]

It is fitting for a king to honor those that his laws contrive, hold folks of religion in reverence, and discretely advance wise and discreet men. He should gladly speak with these men, and ask for diverse needs and things that are good to know and to learn, to inquire honestly and sweetly of things, and to answer them wisely. You must honor the most wise and notable of them, each to his desert. A king should examine the indigence and the needs of poor men and their poverty, and he should help and succor them and relieve their discomforts hastily. It is fitting to the pity that a king should have pity, that he provide for men who know their language, who can easily speak with those who are needy, and such speakers be rightful and piteous, who may in the King's stead, help, comfort, succor, and to make right.

Chapter 9: How a king should be regarding virtues and clothing

Among all other things and virtues that a king should have, he should be prudent and thoughtful about things that may come afterwards and accordingly ordain his actions so that he may more easily support the perils that come afterward. A king should be piteous, shun wrath, and hide and heal the mourning of his heart so that he is not seen as hasty or unwise by a quick manifestation of his wrath.[22] If it happens that a king does any thing unadvisedly, he should repeal it after reflecting discreetly and know his fault with reason. It is a very great virtue and the chief wisdom of knowledge in a king that he can govern himself aright and that he behaves himself well. When a king will do anything openly, he should not be overly hasty or overly slow so that he will not be seen as hasty or slow. O Alexander, desire not the thing that may not endure and that soon passes and that you must quickly forsake and leave. Gather together riches and treasure that may not rot: the permanent life, the realm without end, and joy without grief. Guide all your thoughts all the time to do well and show yourself glorious and brave. Flee the the manners of wild and mad beasts that that cannot have mercy and the fierceness of the lion, and above all things, the filth of the stinking, fleshly lust of a swine. This is used for comparison.[23] You shall not be cruel as a beast that cannot have pity and is without reason, but be merciful among them of whom you have the mastery or lordship. Reflect upon that which may befall, because what peril betides tomorrow, you know not. **Afterwards in this book, gracious lord, you shall find written how you should hold yourself towards rebellious enemies and thieves.** Now, do not give in to your desires for meat, for drink, for the company of women, or for sleeping overly long, as does a swine.[24] **In five things you shall keep yourself from lechery, which is proved by these two verses:**

Speech	sight	touching	kissing	laughing
Colloquium	**visus**	**contactus**	**basia**	**risus**
Sunt	**fomites**	**veneris**	**hec fuge**	**saluus eris**

These are the sources of lechery; shun them and you will be saved. What glory or what valor can happen to you if you accustom yourself to the works of beasts without reason. Believe me without duty, the foolish company of women destroys the body, shortens life, ends all virtues, and transgresses the laws of God. It makes able and brave men like women, soft and weak, in deeds of arms. It is very fitting to a king to be more richly and honestly clothed than all others, that the highness of his dignity may appear in his vesture, and that men set not the less by him but do him due reverence so that his puissance is not marred. A king should be good of speech, soft in word, shun much speech, and speak but little unless he has need. It is better that men desire to hear him rather than that they be sated with his speech, for when a man is troubled and harmed, he hears many words with less will.

Chapter 10: The custom of Jews and how a king should maintain his subjects and namely his merchandise

It is not proper for a king to be overmuch in the company of men in whom little is set store or dishonest persons, for to maintain around him those that are of little value. Such fools and dishonest men make the honor of lordship to fall into contempt. Therefore, there was a fair custom among the Jews; once a year the king would have a parade for his people and his army. He would show himself to his people and the people beneath him, his earls, his noble folk and his barons about him, while sitting on his steed in rich apparel and richly armed. Then he alleviated the great needs that were displayed and told of the diverse misfortunes that betided the realm, and the great contentions and the envies, the concerns, and the needs of the realm. On that day of custom, he gave large gifts, delivered guiltless men out of prison, released grievous debts, and did many other great works of pity. When this was done, then the king would go sit before his people. Soon, one of his counselors would stand before all the folk; among them, they were called attendants or *costeers*, that is to say those that sat beside, for they would sit on every side of him. Then the most wise man of them and the most eloquent in honor of the king would give love and thanks to God that their king governed well the realm of Judah, that God so adorned and endowed the realm with so wise and knowledgeable a king, and because of that, the people of Judah in that time, praised and confirmed obeisance, accord, and stability. Then after he had commended and praised God and the king, he would praise the people, telling of their good virtues and manners in order to win and have their good will. Then he would admonish them by good examples and reasons to obey and honor and humbly serve and truly love their king. The people therefore cried and with high voices they praised and commended their king and his good works and praised him and prayed that God to hold and keep their king's life. At their departing, they went by cities and lineage and praised their king and his works. These people taught their children to love, honor, obey, fear, and value their king, and so increased their own renown. At that time the king was prone to judge the doers of wrong without mercy and so that they would do amiss no more, so that others were thereby chastised. At that time the king would alleviate tributes and release merchants from their rents and defend and keep them in truth. Judah is full of people for that reason. For there come merchants from all lands who are well received there and win much good. There, rich and poor citizens and foreigners may come. There,the tributes of the land and rents increased. It is well that men should shun injuring or doing wrong to merchants for they pass from land to land and expand the regions of kings and realms like as they find. Above that, there is no realm that doesn't have need of some things that are in other lands. Merchants carry those things from land to land and therefore whosoever judges merchants ill in his lordship, he destroys and greatly diminishes the good and the profit of the people. Therefore he is not worthy to have or maintain a realm or a lordship.

Chapter 11: Of the solace of a king

Regarding the majesty of a king, it is suitable that he have privately some true people with him who may gladden him after his troubles and discomforts with diverse instruments of mirth before him to open his heart and comfort him. The soul of a man has delight in instruments of mirth as the senses are kindly nourished, contention, discomfort, and heaviness of fate are put away, and all the body takes strength from them. If in such manner you will play the sport and find solace, three or four days are sufficient, after your pleasing, and it should be done privately and silently. When you will be in such solace, drink but little, make all others drink at their own inclination, pretend to be drunk, and then you may perceive and hear many secret things. This ought not to be done but two or three times a year. In addition, you ought to have some of your household with you so that they may tell what men say or do in your realm. Over the time of solace, it is suitable to a king that he be of demure bearing and fair, that he not laugh overly much, and for him to keep easy countenance, for often laughing puts away the reverence of a prince. This proves true by this verse: **"Per multum risum, potes cognoscere stultum;"** in English, "You may know a fool by his laughing often."

Chapter 12: A king is likened to rain, wind, winter, and summer

There is a likeness between a king and the rain, wind, winter and summer. First is the similarity between a king and the rain: for from the rain comes bad and good. Good comes, for it moistens the herbs, trees, and gardens, and afterwards makes grains and herbs to rise, trees and roots to spring, to blossom, and to seed, and then to bear leaves, flowers, and fruits. From this come many other goods. Also from the rain come many other misfortunes and much harm, such as thunder and lightening; rivers and waters are made to overflow their bounds; beasts and people perish, and much more harm comes from this. Though so much harm comes from this, yet men do yet not abstain from thanking God that sends the rain, from which so much good comes to the land and to the people. The second likeness is between a king and the wind. Good and ill come from the wind. It is good, for it makes grain to grow; it makes fruit to ripen, it makes the rain to fall, and it makes a way for those that pass through the sea. Also, the wind makes many other goods. But there again, diverse perils, ills, and disturbances occur through the wind on land and on the sea. The people in tempests lose their goods and their lives, and from the wind comes the corruption of the air, poisons and other ills are nourished from it. Although all these ills come from the winds, it is not profitable for the people to be without the wind. The third likeness is between a king and winter and summer, for the cold and the heat of the winter and the summer help the springing and the budding of natural things, although many perils and ills comes from them. So it is that a king is like the three things, for the realm is well governed and duly maintained by the good king, and he does many other good things for the people. He does many things because of what is right and the law, and some people are damaged by it, some misled by it, and even with all that he does some are mispaid by it. However, even if the king displeases them, men should not stop their prayers to God that He maintain and sustain their king for the profit of the realm, and to the good of the commons. They ought to thank God that He has given them such a good king.

Chapter 13: Of the prudence of a king

Alexander, see that you are well stored of wheat and of corn and of every manner of grain that is good for living throughout all your realm, so that if a dearth befalls you, you may succor your people by your prudence in their discomfort and suffering. In such a time you shall open your granaries and your storehouses and disclose your cellars so that all of yours may feel the generosity of your bounty and praise the worthiness and discretion of your wisdom. This great knowledge and prudence comforts the realm, saves the people, keeps the cities, and makes the king feared by his subjects.

Chapter 14: Of the mercy of a king

Alexander, ofttimes I have spoken to you and counseled you and I say it again and admonish you that you should not gladly shed the blood of a man, for that belongs to God who knows the thoughts and the secrets of hearts. Hermogenes, the wise scholar, says that when a man slays another, the virtues of heaven will cry to God and say, "Lord, Lord, your servant will be like you." If the slaying is unrightful, God will answer, "Whosoever slays, he shall be slain; vengeance belongs to me and I shall thereof take vengeance." For the death of a guiltless man that is slain will the virtues of heaven cry until that time that vengeance is taken.

Chapter 15: Of three things a king or a prince should be advised of and principally of the third, that a man should keep his word in his vows for any thing

Alexander, remember the deeds and works of your ancestors and keep a paper of their lives and all their acts, for so will you perceive many good things by the examples of their actions. Be advised of the second thing, that you not hold in contempt men that fall from riches into poverty, for he that is now low by poverty, may by fortune be relieved, exalted, and become rich; then he may vex and damage. Do not forget the third thing in any manner. Never break your word that you have given or an alliance confirmed, because that befits untrue men. Over that it is to know that an evil end follows a lie. Though it happens that through a broken word some good should befall at that time, more harm will fall in another time than the good that was gotten before that was due to falseness. Over that, he that breaks his word with falseness and lies will be proclaimed and known.

Alexander, know that by loyalty, truth, and faith the people are unified, cities fulfilled, and lordships maintained. If faith or loyalty is forsaken, then the people and the lordships will be as wild beasts, for among them each one holds himself above the other who is his equal.[25] For these things, fully true emperor; keep your faith, your undertakings, and your oaths in all points though they that you have taken in hand be hurtful. Alexander, know that as Hermogenes says, there are two spirits about you; there is one at your right hand that keeps you, and the other is in your left hand that beholds you. This spirit that sees and perceives all your works, he writes them down if they are not good and shows them to God that made you. This thing only should restrain you and make all men shun evil works. Therefore forswear yourself in no way or break your faith. You must gladly shun swearing for a king should not swear unless it is for a great reason, for a king that would gladly swear does dishonor to his realm. For that is fitting for subjects and to servants, but not to gentlemen or to nobles. Know that the reason for the destruction of the dark realm and of the city was because their kings were accustomed to swearing quickly and easily, for when it befell them to make any oath or other faith, one party would beguile the other and they would break their oaths and their covenants. Because they broke the loyalty that had been established to profit man and health they would not endure any longer the full righteousness of almighty God.

Chapter 16: How a king should advance proud men in armies and the study of clergy to have with him

Alexander, make your bachelors and your young men to be proud to joust in arms, to search for all manner of assaults, to be informed in all manner of battles and of wars. Command many times throughout your realm that all people have their children placed in school and make them to be taught and to study the high and noble sciences that are called liberal sciences, that is to say the free sciences, such as grammar, art, medicine, astronomy, and others. Your prudence owes it to them to find their living. To those that study well you shall give some advancement so that others thereby have a better will to learn. Hire them gladly in their needs, and advance them that are due reward. That shall make the scholars to praise and commend you. That shall make them write of your good works, your generosity, and your bounty, so that your good renown they will make ever to endure. Well maintain the study of the clergy, as it is the worship of the empire, the beauty of the realm, the light of the lordship, and the remembrance of all goods. For by writing books, it makes scholars to be studious; things that are passed, men may know again and in books a man may see them openly. Through the same thing the realm of Greece was enhanced; that made her renown throughout the entire world and to last so long. Certainly that was through the clergy and their study that were so great there and through the very wise philosophers that dwelled in their study. So much was that study in Greece maintained that the young damsels in their fathers' houses knew the courses of the stars and of the years, the reason and the diversity of short and long days and nights, the courses of planets, the measures of circles, the significance of the stars with regard to things to come, the showing of stars and many other related things.

Chapter 17: The prologue of the four cardinal virtues, declaring the virtues of theology and the four manners of goods

Noble and gracious lord, at the beginning of this present book, I said that I would write to your excellence of the four cardinal virtues, understanding that they are not written in Aristotle's aforesaid book. They are written in other good books of Latin, and they are no less profitable than the best thing in Aristotle's book. But first understand, as the Holy Writ says, that there are three principal virtues of theology or divinity, called in Latin, **fides, spes,** and **caritas,** and in English, faith, hope and charity. Faith is a believing of things that our bodily eyes may not see, as in the twelve articles of our common, "**Credo in Deum patrem.**" Hope is a rightful trust for a rightful work put between hopelessness and despair, a presumption of good to come and afterwards to be had, and of ills to come afterwards to be shunned. Charity, as the Master of Sentence says, is "a love, with which God is loved for Himself and our neighbor for God or in God."[26] Also as St. Augustine says, "Charity is the fulfilling of law and of all divine scripture or Holy Writ." That is to say it is the perfect love of our God and of our neighbor. Since that charity is the fulfilling of law and of all divine scripture; though a man has all other virtues, without charity he may not be saved. Therefore, noble lord, never punish the evil doer or the enemy because of hatred or for desire for their goods, but punish them for the love of justice and then right duly punish them, loving their souls by way of charity and hating their evil deeds, and so you shall keep your charity. And if you do the contrary, you pass the bounds of good governance. The great scholar Seneca says, "If you will submit or reveal all things to yourself, submit yourself to reason." Truly, noble lord,you will well govern many people while reason governs you. If you govern yourself after this book, as this is my high trust and prayer to God, after the four cardinal virtues that shall be declared here as I have found written in diverse books, then you shall doubtlessly govern yourself by reason-to God's honor and to yours and to the profit to all of yours and to your well willing over all.

Chapter 18: Of the four cardinal virtues

Cardinal virtues are called principal virtues: the first is called in Latin, **prudencia**, the second, **iusticia**, the third, **fortitudo**, and the fourth is **temporancia**. They are called in French, visonge, or purveyaunce, dreiture, coerance, and temporaunce. They are called in English, wisdom, rightfulness, strength, and temperance. For as much as Latin is the most steadfast language, as often as it is in this present writing of translation, I shall put the Latin names of these four virtues in the place of English, for a man may use diverse English names for every one of them.

Chapter 19: Of the first cardinal virtue that is called Prudencia[27]

At the beginning of the declaration of this virtue, prudence, understand that there are four manners of goods to know: good nature, good fortune, good of the knowledge of clergy, good grace, and good of one's nature includes strength of body, fairness, health, freedom of delivery, and many others[28]. These goods also come to wild beasts as well as men. Good of fortune includes riches of gold, silver, jewels, and other worthy possessions and riches, and it comes to bad men as well as to good, like as to the blessed Job, to the cursed emperor Nero, and to many others since and in our days. Therefore men should set little store for these goods of fortune or of nature as they are not very good, for now they are here and now they are gone. So it is to understand that goods of nature and of fortune are all goods that pertain to sustenance, or adornment, or protection and defense of the body. Goods of the knowledge of clergy are better than the goods of nature or of fortune, for they are goods of the soul; nonetheless, they do make not the soul good of necessity, for the good of knowledge is common to good men and to bad. The best good of all is the good of virtues and grace. Virtue is not only a good, but it is a goodness as well, necessarily making good its possessor and therefore let no man doubt that virtues make the soul the best of all.

Chapter 20: A man should surmount all beasts in virtues, especially in two

It is to be known that as man surpasses all beasts that God ever made in nobleness of nature. So he should surpass them in virtues, namely in two that are the two beginnings and heads of all manners of works of mankind that are to be known: understanding or reason, and will. Therefore every virtue that is done by good understanding or reason is called prudence. Every virtue by which a man does any work duly and rightfully is called justice and pertains to his will, for the rightfulness of works or of deeds comes and rises from rightfulness of will. But of these two goods, it is to say, of the goodness of reason, of the goodness of will, and of their profits, a man is troubled in two manners. In one manner, by the wickedness of fleshly appetites; that is to say, by gluttony and lechery. To refrain from these wicked things, he should have the virtue of temperance. In another manner, men are troubled by the wickedness of heart that comes from foreign things, as the fear a man has of perils, and also of travails, for which it is a needful thing to a man that he be stable and confirmed by the strength of the virtue that goes not out of the way, nor surpasses that which reason gives. This virtue is called strength of courage or of heart; in Latin, as aforesaid, it is called Fortitudo. And as aforesaid, these are the four cardinal virtues that are the known principal or chief virtues. For the other virtues are referred to them to as their chiefs. Though virtue applies to all men, it especially applies to a king and to a prince and to all others that govern and redress any people. Among these virtues that we have named in right order, it should begin with prudence, for by understanding, the will is governed. One's will may not desire anything, unless understanding whows it the will. For as much as prudence is the perfection of good and the virtue of reason, as aforesaid, it is among the virtues touched by prudence, and it is in right order to begin there.

Chapter 21: To have and maintain Prudencia and knowledge

It is that fitting, namely, that a prince has prudence and knowledge, for they are profitable to both him and to his subjects. Therefore Plato, the great philosopher, says that, "Then was the world blessed when wise men reigned and there were wise kings." Solomon says, "**Multitudo sapientum sanitas est orbys terrarum.**" That is to say, "The multitude of wise men is the health of all the world." Valerius, in his seventh book, and Boethius, in his first book, say that the noble scholar Seneca called the world, the golden world, when realms were governed by wise men. Of this, Policratus says in his sixth book that, "Three things made the Romans to conquer land and overcome people, that is to say, knowledge and wisdom proved in arms, high faith, and truth maintained." The same scholar also says in his fourth book, "I may not mind that the emperors of Rome, nor the dukes, were unlettered while their lordship was well governed in its strength." But I do not know how since the light of letters was extended to princes that the strength of all chivalry of princehood and royalty became enfeebled as the known root. But it is no wonder that royalty without wisdom and knowledge may not last. For God, that is Himself knowledgeable, says in the personage of knowledge in the Book of Proverbs, "By me, that is to say, knowledge, kings reigned." Solomon, in his book of wisdom says, "A wise king is the stability of the people." And there he says again, "you kings of the people, if you delight in royal cities and in scepters, love wisdom. That you may reign a long time, love the light of knowledge gladly for all the people you have to govern. A wise judge shall judge his people and their prince shall be stable; an unwise king shall lose his people

and the inhabited cities shall be destroyed by the knowledge of an unwise king."
Over all things the wisdom of a king should govern his law after the law of God
and he should have the law of God and knowledge. The holy prophet, Moses,
wrote about that in the Book of Deuteronomy. After a king is set in the highness
of his realm, he should have the laws of God written and take the examples of the
priests. He should have the same laws at all times with him and read them, so that
he can most fear and dread God and keep and maintain the commandments and
the statutes of His law. Many laws are always good when they do not conflict
with the law of God. By that it appears that a king should be wise so that he not
be called an ape. As Saint Bernard says, "An ape surrounds the fool king that sits
in a seat and therefore if a prince be unlettered, he should, after the counsel of
lettered men, work and govern his realm." Therefore it is written in the Book of
Deuteronomy that, "A king should take example from the law of priests," that is
to say, of lettered man, as Helemaund says.

Chapter 22: Now here begins old stories to prove the aforesaid teaching of prudence true

In order to have and to conquer knowledge and prudence, the old kings
were very covetous, pensive, and desirous which appears well in these stories. In
the third book of Kings we find written, that our Lord appeared on a certain night
to King Solomon as he was sleeping and said to him, "Ask what you will and I
will give it to you." And Solomon said, "You have made your great mercy
towards your servant David, my father, but I am but a little child that can not lie.[29]
I know not my future and your servant is placed here to govern these very great
people that you have chosen. Grant then, to your servant, a heart able to know
and wisdom so that I may judge your people and part the good from the bad. For
who might judge or govern these, your people, that are so great." It pleased God
that Solomon asked such a thing. Then said God to Solomon, "Because you have
asked for such a thing and you have not asked for long life, riches or the conquest

of your enemies, but instead you have asked for wisdom to judge and determine rightfully, I make you what you have requested. And I grant you a wise heart and understanding such that none that have come before you or that come after you will be like you. Beyond that I shall give you that which you have not asked, that is to say, riches, nobleness, and honor, over all the kings that have been before. And if you keep my commandments, I shall give you long life." Whereby it appears that prudence in a prince, unto which prudence belong knowledge, as was aforesaid, pleased God much when Solomon's desire to have knowledge was so much. Therefore these old princes had their masters with them, as Alexander had Aristotle, Nero had Seneca; and Trajan had Plutarch. Of this Policratus says, in his sixth book, that when Alexander was born, King Phillip, who was his father, sent to Aristotle a letter in this form: "King Phillip sends greetings to Aristotle. Know that a son is born to me, but because he is born in your time, I hope that by your teaching and information, he shall be to us suitable to and worthy of the governance of a realm." Of this Policratus says that the Emperor of Rome counseled the King of France and he admonished that he should make his children learn from the knowledge of the clergy, for he says that an unlettered king is like a horned ass.[30]

Chapter 23: The parts of prudence

Cicero says and shows in the second book of rhetoric that prudence has three parts that are to be known: mind, understanding, and foresight.[31] The mind is that by which a man records in himself the things that pass by. By understanding, a man advises himself of things that are now, and by foresight, a man aims for reason in the things that are to come. After the many types of perils, a man remembers and is able to foresee. By his mind, a man should record things that have been before; for as things are in this time, so were they in their time, and just as these things that were then are passed, so shall pass what is now. Therefore a man should little covet or desire the highness, the honor, the joy or the gladness of this world. It behooves us to purchase another life, for we are required to forsake and leave this world. Then, we are not to think of the noblest lords that were before these times as worthy lordships

When the great King Alexander, by conquest, had gotten the empire of the world he then died; and he who had humbled all living people, was laid with other men, dead into the earth. Then said a scholar, "It is much to despise the highness of the world, the royalty of the empire and the honor of riches, for his friendship is but the wrath of grief, his gladness runs always into worse; all is but as a flower in the field." Of Alexander, the mighty emperor, we make a mirror, because for him might not suffice the bread of the world nor the navy of the sea nor to be lord of all. All the lands he conquered from Greece into the east, Darius, the great king he slew and all his people he overcame, but when death cast him down, a little grave of five feet sufficed for his palace, for his hall, and for his robe. Every man take from this example. When Alexander was dead, he was made a grave of gold. Many philosophers came to his interment and one of them said, "In his life Alexander made treasures of gold, but now without any duress, gold makes a treasure of him."

Another said, "Yesterday he was not satisfied with all the world full of precious stones or any palace of gold; today, a little bound of two or three ells suffices him."[32]

The third philosopher said, "Yesterday he had the lordship of all men, today all men have mastery over him."

The fourth said, "Yesterday he led his hosts upon the earth, today they lead him into the earth."

The fifth said, "Yesterday he had earth under his feet, today he is by earth oppressed."

The sixth said, "Yesterday he had particular friends, but today he has them all alike."

Therefore no man should have pride of highness, of lordship, of riches, or of power, for they may not last long. Beyond that, God does not hold much of earthly highness and so it seems well, for God gives lordship and highness to cursed men as well as to good men. However, goodness comes from the royalty and riches of good men, while many lusts and much mischief come from the lordship of cursed men. That appeared well in Nero to whom God granted the lordship of the entire world and the empire of Rome, of whose majesty, felony, and cruelty men find written. Nero had the wise scholar Seneca as his master; this worthy scholar, Seneca, had long abode and he had hope of a great reward for his hard work and his good service. Nero said to him, "Chose in what tree you will be hanged from, for that is the reward of your hard work." Seneca asked him in what manner he had deserved death and such reward. Then Nero made a sharp sword to flourish over Seneca's head and Seneca feared death and turned aside his head at the threat of the sword. Then said Nero, "Master, why turn your head from the sword?" Seneca answered, "I am a man and the dread of death grieves me." Nero said to him, "I am like a child and I fear you now as much as a child, wherefore I may not live in ease while you live." Then Seneca said to him, "Since I must die, grant me that I may chose a manner of death." Nero said to him, "Chose hastily the death and tarry you not." Then he made a bath to be ordained for him and in the bath placed both of his arms to let blood. He bled so much that in the bath he died. Boethius, in the Book of Consolation, says that this caused Nero to slay his brother, and he killed his mother, made her to be opened so that he would see and know how he was borne and fed in the womb. The physicians and leeches reproved him for the death of his mother, for it was against reason and nature that the son should slay his mother and who suffered great grief because of him, and who with much travail nourished him.[33] Then Nero said, "Make me with child and to bear a child that I may know how great the grief and pain was that my mother had with me." And the physicians said, "That may not be, for it is against nature." Then Nero said them, "If you make me not with child, I shall make you all die a cruel death." Later, they gave him privately a little toad in a drink and by craft, made it grow in his belly. His belly swelled and grew large such that he couldn't bear it, a thing against nature. Therefore, he determined that he was with child. The physicians made him eat such meat that made the little toad grow according to its nature and said to him, "Since you will conceive and bear a child, a woman with child must eat meat." It befell that through the growing of the toad, so great was his dolor that he could no longer endure it.Therefore he said to his physicians, "Hasten you the time of my child bearing, for the distress is so strong to me that only with need can I inhale my breath." Then they gave him a drink to cast it out and he cast out a toad that was strongly foul and hideous. Nero beheld his child and thereof had horror, and he marveled of such a shape. The physicians said to him, "The shape is such because you would not abide the time of childbearing." From that time he commanded them to keep his child and to nourish it well, and it was enclosed in a vault of stone. This Nero slew St. Peter and St. Paul and thereafter he thought of and marveled at the burning of Troy. Because he would know how great the fire-blast was, he set the city of Rome afire and it burned seven days and seven nights. The city was ablaze and it surpassed the fair tower that was great in height. Nero rejoiced greatly for the beauty of the fire-blast. He was prone to fish with gilded nets. When those of Rome saw this insanity, they could endure it no longer. They assailed the tyrant, chased, and pursued him out of the city. When he perceived that he might not escape, he ran to a stake and stuck himself through the body, and died. Then, he that had the title of emperor of all the world and lordship in his life had so little honor after his death that no man would bury him, but he was left to be devoured wild beasts and flying fowls. In an ill time the lordship of Solerne, there as the day dawns, or the Baillie of Galerne, there as the night fell, was not sufficient for Nero. After all this glory, a foul death befell him. All men have it in mind that from death there is no resort. Therefore it appears well that God grants the highness of honor heartily to bad men as well as to good men. Therefore no man should pride himself due to highness, or riches, empire, royalty, lordship, nor earthly honor, for they will not wait or endure, but soon will pass, like flowers they shall fade.

Therefore St. Augustine says in the book of true innocence, "If you vaunt the riches that flourished from the nobility of your ancestors, of beauty of body, of strength, or of the honors that the people give you, behold yourself, that you are earth and into earth you will go. Remember those men that were before you that have been in the beauty of glory. Where are they that were surrounded with the great power of citizens and where are the wise legislators that might not be surpassed in knowledge? Where are they that held the great feasts and made great banquets? Where are they that nourished the high priced horses? Where are those that led the great hosts? Where are the mighty warriors, the dukes, and the tyrants? They are all turned into powder and into ashes and in empty words only is their memory made. Behold their graves! Determine if you can who was servant, who was lord, who was rich and who was poor. Discern if you can the person of the king from the person of the knave, the strong from the feeble, and the fair from the foul. Therefore remember you of your nature that you pride yourself not and from that, take heed if you will keep yourself."

Chapter 24: Understanding: that is the second part of the virtue of prudence

As I said before, the second part of prudence is understanding. This virtue advises a man of things that are now. Among all things that are to be understood, it is principally necessary that a man know himself, for other things he suffers in vain to know that he will forget.

Therefore, as St. Jerome tells us, in old times when the princes of Rome returned from battles where they had had victory, the Romans made three manners of honors. The first was that all the people proceeded towards the Prince with great gladness. The second was that the prisoners and hostages that were taken in the battle should follow the prince's chair on their feet with their hands bound behind their backs. The third was that the prince should be clothed in Jupiter's coat, their god, sitting in a chair that four white horses drew. But even as much as the Romans willed that the Prince should not forget his honor, he must suffer three dishonors in the same day. The first was that there, as the prince sat in his chair, a bondsman of foul condition to signify that every man of the people should have hope to have the same glory of a prince or of an empire through prowess and vassalage. The second dishonor was that the bondsman sat with the prince on a stool, giving him blows and strokes, saying in Greek, "Notisclotos," that is to say: know yourself, be not proud of so high worship and remember that you are mortal. The third dishonor was that every man might, without pain or reproof, speak against the prince for that day.

In this way, Julius Caesar, the strong warrior, when he came to Rome again after the conquest of his enemies, received many reprisals and indignities from the people and he never took vengeance upon them. David the prophet said of men that are honored and know not themselves, "**Homo, cum in honore esset, non intellexit, etc.,**" which is to say, "When a man is in honor, he does not understand, he is likened to wild beasts without reason as he is made like them." Also David says, "**Nolite fieri sicut equus et mulus, in quibus non est intellectus, etc.,**" which is to say, "Be not as a horse and a mule, in whom there is no understanding."

Chapter 25: Of the third part of prudence that is called foresight

The third part of prudence is foresight by which a man is advised of things that are to come. Though a man has never so good a fortune, he needs foresight. The more rich and able a man is, the more he should consider this. Of this,

Cicero, the wise scholar tells us in the *Book of Questions* of one Dionysus, the cruel tyrant and the king of the realm of Sicily.[34] One of his friends that was called Damocles said, "God has endowed you much with grace; you are rich and wealthy with great lordships, castles, towers, power of the people, fair horses, clothes of silk, and a rich family. No man is the like you." And the King answered him, "Would you like to experience my fortune?" "Yes," said the other gladly. Then the King ordained that Damocles be set in a fair bed of gold and he had a fair table, full of precious meats, set before him. Also, he made fair young women to stand him before him and made them serve him. When he was in all these delights, the King commanded that men should hang over his head and his neck a sword of sharp steel, such that nothing held the sword except one horse's hair. Then he that sat in the delights beheld the peril in which he was set. For fear of death, he forgot the delights, so that he paid no attention to the bed of gold, to the delicious meats, or to the fair young women that served him. Then the King said, "Such is all my life that you so much praised." "I pray you," said Damocles, "let me pass hence."

All the days of our life we are in great peril, for three enemies we war with. Days and nights they make their assaults in us: the world that draws us to greed, the flesh that chases us to lechery, and the Devil that assails us with pride and envy. He is much a fool and ignorant that does not fear nor seek help in so cruel a battle. Therefore, Job says that chivalry is man's life on earth. While we live in the manner of knights, we fight, for when this life takes an end, there shall be no more chivalry. Whoever thinks of his death all the time will have victory over these enemies. Therefore Solomon says, "Fair child, remember that you will die and you will sin never more." The best words that were ever found are that you will die.

Chapter 26: That prudence is to be much praised; these following reasons prove well

Cicero, speaking of prudence in a fair manner, says, "If you desire to have prudence, you will lead your life by reason." And you will consider all things after their nature and not after what men say, for many things seem good and are not and others seem not good and are good. All is not gold that shines as gold. You shall not much hold nor praise the goods that soon must pass. The good that God has given you, you should not keep it as another man's good, but to spend and use as your own. If you have embraced prudence you will never be unstable, but after that, your time and your things will suggest that you be guided and reflective, so that for every need that you undertake, you can be able and according. For it is not the hand, now at length or as a straightened palm that then closes into a fist that is moved or changed. It belongs and is proper to prudence to examine and to test one's counsel and not to fall in error or falseness by easy credence. You should not decide things that are in doubt, but until the time when you are very sure, you shall abide. Give not lightly your sentence, for it is not always true which seems true. Often truth has a face of lying and often a lie has the color of truth, as he that is a friend often shows a drooping countenance, and the liar and deceiver shows a fair countenance.[35] If you desire to be wise and to work by prudence, consider the fear of what may befall so that nothing may befall suddenly. Whosoever is wise says not, "I didn't think that this should happen to me", but, "I knew well that this might happen to me, and therefore, I have provided against it." For each thing you will do, make sure that it is good to begin and then you must consider what end it will have, for without a good end, little is worth a good beginning. Whosoever is wise and considerate will not beguile, nor be beguiled. Receive not swift thoughts that are like a dream, for if you delight in such thoughts, when you have thought all, mourning and anger you will reign. Let your thoughts be stable, certain, and true, and let your word be not in vain, but let it be of solace or of benefit. You shall praise and commend scarcely and seldom, but you will blame more scarcely, more prudently and more seldom. He is to be reproved that overly and too often praises, as he that dispraises and blames beyond moderation. Too much praise is suspected of being a lie and too much criticism is suspected of malice. You may witness this for truth but not for friendship, for a friend is to love, and truth is much more. Therefore he is an unwise man that gives an audience or gifts to poets or any such liars, for they praise their givers be they ever so vicious. Whosoever gives them any good breaks the Statutes of Kilkenny, and he is accursed by eleven bishops as the same statutes mention.[36] Promise nothing suddenly, for when you hasten to promise you will give more. If you are wise in heart you must think and know of three times: things that are now to be ordained, things to come to provide for, and those that are passed to remember. Whosoever thinks nothing of things past, he shall be called a dolt and a fool. Whosoever reckons nothing of what may befall, he will fall into sudden mischief. Whosoever reckons not what he does shall soon come to evil exploits. Consider things good and evil that might happen so that you might better sustain adversity and better maintain prosperity. Do not always be in travail and in thoughts, but sometimes in joy and solace without sin. When you are at rest, keep yourself from idleness, for the Holy Writ says, "**Otiositas inimica est anime, et radyx viciorum.**" which is to say, "Idleness is the enemy of the soul and the root of vices " The wise and the well-governed man, when he will withdraw himself from great concerns, should have nothing to do with idleness or folly. He has needs to attend to, judgments to determine, severity to lessen, wrongs to redress, and strifes to ease; all that he ought to do, soon he perceives and he fears to do amiss. He fulfills his good deeds and works without chiding, vaunting, or making great noise; such is the wise man's guise and his manners. Let not the authority of the speaker move you; take no heed of what person the speaker is, but think about what he means. "Many a poor man shows wisdom and reason and many a prince shows great folly without reason." Also, have no care to please all men but only good men. Do not care to be praised by fools and shrews, but by good and wise men. It is a great honor and praiseworthy to displease bad men and shrews, and to praise them and to be praised by them is blameworthy and full of reproof. You should desire such things that good men desire and praise. Desire not the thing that may not come to you. When you are in prosperity, think upon adversity and in time of peace, of war, for it is too late when you are taken. The wise man will not be mistaken, for he will consider beforehand. It belongs to the office of prudence to redress the deeds if all other virtues; to it belongs to show what, when, and how something is to be done; to it belongs to foresee in that our works to God be acceptable, profitable to us, and not wrongful to our neighbors, that God be glorified in our works, that we be rewarded, and that good examples be given to our neighbors. Also, to the office of prudence, it belongs to act according to true opinion and not according to the opinion of diverse people. Also, to the office of prudence, it belongs to be stable and not variable. Solomon says, "A holy man in wisdom abides as the sun and a fool changes as the moon." Also prudence shuns dishonesty in privacy as well as in open places, also it wisely acts in prosperity, rather than in adversity. It is to be known that he that commits mortal sins does himself seven great follies. First, he blinds himself, for the Book of Wisdom says, "The malice of sinners blinds themselves." The second is that he binds himself to the Devil, as Job says, "**Misit in rethe pedem suum**" ("He has put his foot in the net"). But as Gregory says, "He will not, when he wills it, draw it out." The third is that as an angry man he inflicts himself with an incurable wound by his own hands, for Solomon says, "By malice he has slain his soul." Sin is the death of the soul for it separates man from God, which is his life. The fourth is that he casts his goods away, for whosoever does a deadly sin has lost all of the good deeds that ever he did until the time that he returns to a good life. Also, the good that he does in that sin are not truly good, for they are not meritory to him. The fifth is that he goes away from the maker of all things, for Hosea, the holy prophet, says, "**Ve eis quoniam recesserunt a me**" ("Woe to them, for they have left me"). The sixth is that he presumes to make war on almighty God, which war would soon be ended, if the mercy of God would allow it. The seventh folly is that he shuts the gates of Paradise to himself and sells the Kingdom of Heaven for a little price, as Esau did, that for a little potage sold the right of his inheritance.

Chapter 27: The second cardinal virtue that is called in Latin, Iustitia, and in English, rightfulness or right

The law of Emil expounds this virtue of justice, in this manner in Latin, **"Iusticia est constans et perfecta voluntas, ius suum vnicuique tribuens."** That is to say, "Right is a steadfast and perfect will, giving to every man what is rightful." St. Augustine says that there are two parts of justice that are to be known: "Give up harm and do good." The prophet says of this, **"Declina a malo, et fac bonum."** And Christ says in the gospel, **"Primum querite regnum dei et iusticiam eius,"** which is to say, "Ask first for the kingdom of God and His rightfulness." In another place, He says, **"Beati qui esuriunt et siciunt iusticiam,"** which is to say, "Blessed be those that hunger and thirst for right." Some scholars divide the virtue of justice into five parts: first, in obedience in suffering, in correction of the subject, for equity among peers, and in truth and faith, which pertains to all men. Seneca describing justice says, **"Iusticia diuina lex est, et vinculum societatis humane."** That is to say, "Right is the law of God and a bond of men's fellowship." For the law of God charges you to do to your neighbor as you would have him do to you. If you desire the virtue of justice, love God, do profit to all men, and discomfort no man. You will leave alone evil men that would annoy you, that they will not move true men to discomfort or chasten or disturb. You shall punish evildoers, which action pertains to the virtue of justice. He consents to wicked men that which wickedness will not destroyIn the Book of Kings, the scripture tells us that Eli the priest was a very good holy man, but because he slackly reproved and did not chastise his sons by strictness of the law, they were wicked and lecherous men; for that God took grievous vengeance. They were killed in battle for their sins and thirty thousand of God's people died with them by an assault of disbelieving men. Also, the ark of God, in which the Jews so much delighted, was stolen away. Therefore, when Eli heard the new tidings, he fell out of the chair where he sat, his neck was broken, and there he died. The good King David, the worthy and the brave, the renowned of force and of virtue, of knowledge and of bounty, of whom God says, "I have found a man after my heart," for as much as he was overly tender of his children and chastised them not in their young age, he found them proud, unruly, fierce, and presumptuous afterwards when they were fully grown; so they would have reigned, with their father living. One of them, that was called Absalom, chased David out of the realm and lay with his father's concubines. War continued a long time between the father and the son until God abated the wicked presumption of the tyrant, for he was killed in battle and his men were discomfited. That God punishes them that chasten not their subjects, I think it appears many times by diverse English captains of Ireland in the past and present, whose negligence in not punishing their nations and subjects have destroyed themselves, their nations, and their lands. It avails nothing nor is it necessary to tell the names of these captains, and also it is heinous and perilous to repeat them. So for those three causes, I leave that matter and also, the truth to tell, in case I should be killed in this part, for in his proverbs, Solomon says, "Truth begets hatred, and good service begets friends." Therefore, says the apostle in his epistle that he wrote to the four Galatians, "I am", he says, "made an enemy unto you by telling to you the truth." These days the truth is misspoken; these days, the truth is withheld, bound and imprisoned, for as Matthew Paris says, hardly is found the man that would say it.[37] Therefore Seneca says a notable word for princes and rich men to know; he says thus, "I shall show you what it is, that thing that he lacks that has all riches in possession. I say that they lack men that would say to them the verities, or the truth." In these days truth is, on every side, impugned, so that it is often necessary to follow after the word of Isaiah who says, "**Veritas cecidit in**

platea." That is to say, "Truth has fallen to the payment." Truth casts down, when any unrightfully thing is preferred to truth, but truth, that is so now despised and little is set by it, in a coming time will deliver his lovers and condemn his enemies after the word of our Savior, who says, "You will know truth and truth will deliver you." Matthew Paris says, "As the false penny is to the true, so the false man is to the true man." Also he says, "We should do truth unto all men." Therefore St. Augustine says, "Every man that lies does ill and wickedly, and in that he lies, no lying man keeps truth or faith." Solomon says, "A lying man is hateful unto God", for when all treasure is tried, truth is the best. Now I leave this manner of matter and speak further of chastising bad men and trespassers. I say that governors of the people should correct bad men so that they may not abide long, for a poet says, "**Qui non vult dum quid, postea forte nequibit.**" That is to say, "Whosoever will not when he can, he will not when he will." The great poet Ovid says, "**Pryncipijs obsta**" ("Withstand the beginning"), for lighter is a fresh wound to heal than one that has festered. While an oak is a young spire, it may be wound into a band to tie twigs, but when it is a grown tree, a hundred oxen may hardly bend it. Solomon says, "**Qui parsit virge odit filium**" ("Whoever spares the rod hates the child"). Whosoever spares the thief, he slays the true man. That a prince should execute the dint of sword on his enemy, especially on false people, and that he should not postpone the hour of fortune, these following stories show. The first Book of Kings tells us that our Lord God anointed King Saul upon Israel, placed him in the way, and said, "Go and slay the sinners of Amalek and you will fight against them until they are dead."[38] Saul went forth, took Agag, the King of Amalek as his prisoner, killed the people, and Saul's people made prey of the best oxen and sheep. Then came the holy prophet Samuel to King Saul and said, "Why have you not heard the voice of our Lord, for you have done ill in the sight of God; and for as much as you have put away the word of God, God has cast you away so that you will not be king of Israel." So while Saul was alive, he was dethroned and the holy David was anointed king of Israel. Moreover, because Saul did not fulfill the execution by dint of sword in Amalek, as he was charged, he was troubled with the Devil. The hands of this holy prophet killed the cursed King Agag. Also Dares, a scholar that was at the siege of the noble city of Troy, and told the story of it, tells and affirms for truth that at the second battle between the Trojans and the Greeks, that after Monestus, the Duke of Athens, had wounded this noble knight, Hector, son of Priam the King of Troy, slew in the same day, more than a thousand knights. By which actions, he (Hector) brought the host of Greeks into a state of such great feebleness that none of them had the heart to defend themselves, nor had their king Agamemnon power to set himself to battle. Therefore the Trojans virtuously pursued the Greeks flying swiftly into their tents and as men that had victory, they burned the Greek ships and they packed up their gold, silver, armor, and jewels with them. This was the day that an end was made of the battle. The Trojans might have been victors forever, but, oh, how light blinded the Trojans' eyes and especially Hector's who might have avoided the undoing of himself and all of his. For that day the Trojans were so mighty that all the Greeks that were there against them, might have been killed. Discretion in a wise man should not be praised when that man is in high need or set in mortal peril and good fortune befalls him such that he may suddenly be delivered of such need or peril and he will not accept the grace that fortune gives him. But as soon as a gracious man forsakes that grace, within the hour, he will never be able to return to it; so it befell the unhappy Hector in that day in which, with great honor, he might have had victory over his enemies. When all his enemies flew fast from him, then Ajax, the son of Telamon the King, a brave knight, strongly made an assault on Hector. But as they spoke together in battle at that time, Hector knew him well and that he was his near cousin; he was glad that he saw his cousin Ajax, he put his arms away and he made great cheer to please his cousin more entirely. He prayed him to see the fair city of Troy honestly within and disported awhile with his great kinsman. Then Ajax lowly prayed Hector, that if he loved him so much, as he said, that he would make and procure that the Trojans for that day would cease battle against the Greeks and to follow the chase no more, but go home to the city. Hector thereto granted the truce and that day it was proclaimed by trumpet; the Trojans left the battle with great dolor and went home. This was such a light reason for the Trojans to stop their intention for victory that day, and they never came near that point again. But, a short time later, this brave knight Hector was killed, the people were all killed and driven out and the excellent city of Troy was forever subverted and destroyed. This city, as Dares says, was three days journey in length and as much in breadth; the walls of it were of marble and two hundred cubits in height with many towers of great height above the walls. Every house of the city was made of marble and they were sixty cubits in heights. The siege of Troy lasted ten years. The first cause of all the war, now shortly to tell, was this: Pelias, King of Thessaly in Greece, sent a brave and bold knight, Jason, his brother's son, with a fresh fellowship, into the Isle of Colchis to win the ram's fleece of gold that belonged to Aeëtes the king. This Jason sailing thither landed at Troy to refresh himself and his men. Knowledge of the fresh array of Jason and his men came to Laomedon, the king of Troy. This king, having envy, sent by message to Jason that he should leave his land without delay. Jason did so and said, "Courtesy would not have the king to harm strangers; hospitality would be better. And peradventure, as this year passes, I shall land here whether that he wills it or not." And so he did and he killed the king, he burned Troy, and he ravished the king's daughter. But Priam, son to Laomedon and father to Hector, restored Troy so excellently, as I said before, that it would never have been taken had no treason been done. It is to be known that Rome, Venice, Italy, Lombardy, France, England, and many other provinces were and are inhabited, for the most part, by the people that escaped out of this noble city, the new Troy, when it was won.

Noble and gracious lord, consider these two stories written before. Since God and our king have granted you power, execute openly, with the sharp edge of your sword, false enemies, traitors, rebels, and killers of true men when they fall into your hands. This is to be said by rigor of the law and by dealing strokes, keep in mind what I said before of the poet, "Withstand the beginning." For as a spark of fire raises a huge fire able to burn a realm, so rises from the root of a false enemy; open traitors, other rebels, many wicked weeds soon grow, so that all true men in the land grieve sorely. Therefore, when they fall into your hands, raze them all out by the root, as the good gardener does the nettles. I know well the root of the nettle, one doughty O'Dennis, father of him that is now, from whom sprang the weeds that as much in my time have destroyed the county of Kildare as all Irish men of Ireland thereafter. [39] This nettle in point was to have been raised out by the root, when you, gracious lord, worshipfully won the castle of Lei out of the false nettles' hands, in the year of our Lord, Jesus Christ, 1420. And you delivered the same castle, to the lord thereof, the aforesaid Earl of Kildare. In the same year the same false nettles easily got it again.

Chapter 28: A prince should not trust his enemy

Bernard says, **"Debilitas inimici non est pax, sed ad tempus treuga,"** what is to say, "The feebleness of the enemy is not a peace, but a truce for the time." And if you trust that your enemy thinks not the same subtlety that you think, you put yourself in danger, and therefore Solomon says, **"Non confidas inimico tuo in eternum."** That is to say, "Never trust in your enemy." Touching this matter, I find this written in this manner. Going one way, two men accompanied each other. One was a philosopher and a faithful man; the other man was a Jew. The philosopher rode upon a mule that he had fostered at his own pleasing and carried with him all necessities for a man that should ride; the Jew went on his feet and had nothingto eat or any other necessities. They talked together, and the philosopher said to the Jew, "What is your law and what is your faith?" The Jew answered, "I believe that in heaven is one God which I honor, and I will good towards all men that accord with me in my faith, in my law, in my belief, and that have good will towards me. Whosoever is in conflict with my law, it is lawful for me to slay him, to take his money from him and to take his wife and his children also. And above all things I am accursed in my law if I keep faith and truth with him, or help him, or do him mercy, or spare him of anything." After this the Jew said to the philosopher, "I have now showed you my law and my faith, now show yours to me." The philosopher said, "This is my faith and my law. First I desire good to myself, to my children and to my kin, and I will no harm towards any creature of God who holds to my law or to any other. I believe that mercy and right is to be done to every living man, and no wrong pleases me, and it seems to me that if harm is to befall any man, it touches and harms me. I desire prosperity, health, solace, felicity, and goodness to all men in common." Then said the Jew, "And what if a man has done you wrong or offence?" The philosopher said, "I know that in Heaven is one God, good, rightful, and wise, and nothing may be hidden from Him; He rewards good and bad men after their deserts." The Jew answered, "Why do you not keep your law, and why do you not confirm your faith in doing deeds?" And he answered, "How shall I it do?" The Jew answered him, "See me here, a man afoot, hungry, thirsty, and worn by hard work, and you ride yourself at ease." "You speak truth," said the philosopher, and he soon alighted down from the mule, opened his pouch, and gave him meat and drink. Afterwards he set the Jew on his mule. Soon after the Jew saw that he was well arrayed and that the mule was swift; he smote the mule with the spurs and left the philosopher far behind. Therefore he cried, "Alas, I am perplexed." The Jew rested the mule a little and said, "I showed you my law and its condition, and I will confirm it." Then hastily he drove the mule forth. This philosopher said, "Leave me not in this desert to be killed by lions, or other wild beasts, or die of hunger, discomfort, thirst, or some other mischief; but have mercy for me as I had for you." The Jew did not deign to look backwards to behold him; he would not hear and he did not stop until he was passed out of his sight. And when the philosopher was so in despair without succor, he remembered his perfection and

50

his faith and of what he had said to the Jew, that in Heaven was one rightful judge, God, from whom nothing may be counseled or hid. Then he lifted up his head to God and said, "Lord God, you know that I believe in you, and in your law, and in your commandments; I praise you and magnify you. And therefore confirm your honor against this Jew." When he had said thus, he went not far thence and there he found the Jew fallen down from the same mule which had broken the Jew's thigh and hurt his neck, and the mule was standing on the Jew's belly. When the mule saw his lord that had nurtured him, he knew him and went to him. The philosopher leaped upon the mule and departed from the Jew, who abode there in peril of death. The Jew cried, "O fair brother, have mercy for me, for I die. Keep your law, for God has granted you victory." Then he began to blame the philosopher more reproachfully, "You sin wickedly if you leave me without mercy." Then the philosopher said, "You sinned cursedly when you left me without mercy." The Jew answered, "Reprove me not of past trespasses, for I said to you that such was my law and my faith in which I was nourished and in which I found all my ancestors nourished and my elders therein continue to be." Therefore, noble and gracious lord, consider that neither your Irish enemies nor their ancestors that were with need were true to you or to your father, more than you were stronger than they were. Witness yourself that Arthur MacMurrough was not true or held no peace longer than your father's life for all the great oaths that he swore.[40] This aforesaid philosopher had mercy on the Jew and made him ride behind him into the place where he desired to be among his own people. Not long after, the Jew died and when the King of the City heard of this matter, he sent for the philosopher and made him his private counselor for that merciful work and for the bounty of his law.

**Chapter 29: The manner of correction that a prince should use against
his subjects**

It is to be known that correction should come from love, according to the
Holy Writ: **"Ego quos amo arguo et castigo"** ("I blame and chasten those men
that I love"). But some princes and judges would correct those men namely for
whom they have envy, whose correction is nothing but a hostile persecution.
Isaiah, the holy prophet says, **"Egredietur virga de radice Iesse."** That is to say,
"A rod shall come out of the root of Jesse." "Jesse" is simply to say, "a burning,"
for from a burning of love should come out the rod of correction. Therefore you
shall not correct your subjects as an enemy, but as a brother. Correction without
mercy is a blind madness and like a blind archer who goes to smite a deer and hits
a man, as Lameth did who intended to shoot a wild beast and smote Cayme and
killed him. In olden times the love of justice and rightfulness of judgment reigned
in pagan princes much more than it does now in our Christian princes. As
Valerius says, a king that was called Cambyses found that one of his judges
whom he had set to judge his people gave a false sentence.[41] Wherefore this king
commanded that he be flayed and he covered the seat with his skin where he was
wont to sit when he judged. And Cambyses commanded that the judge's son,
who became the judge after him, should sit in the same seat and judge in order
that he should have a reminder of the pain of his father, upon whose skin he sat.
In this manner he found a new pain by which he cleverly chastised false judges.
Aristotle praises the virtue of justice and says that it is the fairest virtue of all
virtues, shining more brightly than the daystar. Therefore without this virtue may
no prince rightfully reign, for the power of a prince that does not rightfully judge
is likened to a sharp sword in a madman's hand. All other virtues are valuable to
those men that have them, but the rightfulness of a prince reaches to all those that
are subjects to him. Therefore the people of Judah said that the rightfulness of a
prince is more profitable to his subjects than plenty of meat and drink. Helinand,
who wrote stories about the Romans, tells in his book that Trajan, the emperor of

Rome, leaped up to his horse and was ready to go to battle. There came forth a widow and held him by the foot and she complained dolefully and with weeping, prayed to him that he would do her right concerning those men who had slain her son, thought he was but an innocent. She said, "Sire, you are emperor and I have suffered a cruel wrong." The Emperor answered, "When I come again, I shall do what you desire." She said, "And what if it happens that you never come again?" "My successor will do you right." She answered, "What will it avail you, the good that another man, your successor, will do? You are my doctor and you will receive a reward for what you deserve. It is wrong and deceitful not to pay the debt that is owed. Your successor will be bound for himself and to those who suffer wrong. Another man's rightfulness may not save you. It will be an honor to your successor, and it will befall him well, if he may save his own." To these words went the Emperor's heart, tender with pity that he took from her words. Straightaway he descended from his horse and sat in judgment, and instantly he did full right to the widow. And therefore the Romans made an image of him in the middle of the street to show how he did right to the widow, before he went to war upon felons and enemies of the empire. At another time it happened that Trajan's son rode an undaunted horse that trod over a widow's son in the street until he died. She made a complaint to the emperor and thereof asked for right. He took his own son and gave him to the widow for her son who was dead to do her will with him. Therefore it was cried by the senators of Rome in their Senate, in an audience of all the people, "No man strives more than Caesar Augustus, nor is any man better than Trajan." Our Christian princes should read much and be ashamed when they do not do right to the people or slackly and slowly amend their wrongs, as well as when they delay when justice should be done freely to poor as well as to rich, due to favor or hate, or sell justice for pennies and save guilty men and damn guiltless men. Those men are likened to the Jews, the cruel felons that saved Barabas, the thief and a murderer of men, and crucified Jesus, the very Savior. The bad princes shall be deeper in the torments of Hell than the bad subjects, and deeper, the Christian princes than the pagan princes if they do not do right to all men. If they do well, they will have more rewards. It is written about this in the *Book of Wisdom*, "Mercy will be granted to the little people, but the mighty and strong men will suffer torment more strongly." There was once a hermit that all the time prayed to God that He would show him of what merit he was and to what degree. At last a voice from Heaven answered him, "You are of the same merit, before God, as Gregory the Pope." Then said the hermit, "Alas, in an ill time I came into this desert, in an ill time I saw this hermitage and in discomfort, poverty, and very great sufferance I have been so many years. Now I am but like Gregory the Pope that has such great honor, reverence, and riches. He has such high glory and power that all the world kneels and is subject to him." When this hermit demeaned himself so, he fell nigh in despair. The voice of the angel said, "You are a doddered fool and are overly confident. How dare you make comparisons between Gregory and yourself? You love more the cat that you have than Gregory loves in all the world." By this it appeared very well that riches and highness of the world does not take away good virtues. But the great lords are to be praised more that lead and govern their subjects, the people, by knowledge and virtues than powerful men that have nothing to govern or to maintain but themselves. This Gregory, as the story says, because that he had heard of Trajan the Emperor and that he was full of right, was doleful that so rightful a prince had perished. And he prayed to God intently with his entire heart that if it pleased Him, He should take this emperor out of Hell and save him. An angel said to Gregory, "At this time God has heard your prayer. Trajan is saved, but from hence forth bid you no more such prayers." O Lord God, you love so much the virtue of justice. Because of it, you had mercy for a pagan and he shall have in Heaven the bliss that never ends, for you granted justice to him. And to that same bliss, Jesus Christ, Heaven's king, brings us. Amen.

Chapter 30: Here ends the book of justice and begins the third virtue that is called in Latin, fortitude and in English, strength of heart, boldness, manhood or hardiness

The third cardinal virtue is called fortitude. St. Augustine says in the book of *Moribus Ecclesie*, "**Fortitudo vero est amor facil omnia tollerans propter id quod amatur.**"[42] That is to say, "Fortitude is a love which easily suffers all things for the thing that is loved." The gloss upon the Gospel of Matthew says, "**Fortitudo est firmitas animi contra molestias seculi.**" That is to say, "Fortitude is a steadfastness of the soul against the grievance or heaviness of the world." Cicero in the *Second Rhetoric* says, "**Fortitudo est considerata periculorum suscepcio et laborum perpessio.**" That is to say, "Fortitude is a considered understanding of peril and a sufferance of travail." Also Cicero says that, "**Fortitudo est magnarum rerum appeticio et humilium contempcio et cum racione humilitatis laborum perpessio.**" That is to say, "Fortitude is a desire for great things, a despising of lowly things, and a sufferance of travail with the profit of reason." By this virtue of fortitude, a man may sustain tribulations, adversities and hard chances, without faintness of heart, and bear well his good fortunes without any pride. By this virtue the heart of a man is so much stabilized that not for a chance is it grieved, but it holds him steadfast and strong in all perils, good and ill, not changing his heart. All the holy martyrs and worthy men of arms that were before us had this virtue highly. Cicero says that whosoever has the virtue of fortitude will live with great trust, freely and without fear. It is much to man's great courage, not to flinch, but to stand stable and yield the end of his life without fear. If you have this virtue of fortitude, you will never say that wrong is done to you, but of your enemy you will say he grieved me not, but he had will to grieve. He that is wise and brave has the virtue of fortitude properly and some men call him a courageous or a virile man. Such a courageous man will say ill of no man in his in the presence or his absence. He will battle openly, for deceit and treachery belongs to him that is faint of heart. Then he that does not desire great peril, as does the foolhardy, will be deemed brave, courageous, and not overly fearful as the faint coward is. Aristotle, in the fourth book of *Ethics*, describes the brave in this manner: "The brave does not put himself in peril by small things that help little, for such do these fools that so much. The fools praise things that are worth little that they put themselves in peril of life for them. And to love much a thing of little value pertains to a cowardly heart. But for a great thing and of great price, the brave gladly puts himself in peril of life, such as for the common profit of the city, country, or a realm, to save holy church, or to enhance the worship of God. In such cases the brave boldly puts his life in peril, and he would rather live in honor than to live without virtue in dishonor." So did the good kings, princes, earls, barons, and knights that came before us; as did King David, Samson, Judas Maccabees and his brothers, Arthur, Charles of France, the good Prince Edward, James, your grandfather, Maurice Fitz Gerald, Robert Stevens' son, Raymond le Gros, John de Courcy, and many others of the conquest of Ireland.[43] The brave gives more gladly than receives and he rewards greatly; among high men and lords he conducts himself highly and among the common people, he conducts himself modestly so that he may accord them all. The brave intermeddles with few things; he takes few needs in hand and they shall be of great nobleness and of great renown, because to intermeddle in all things is characteristic of him that has a low heart and little virtue. The brave or the manly does not do anything in secret for he will do nothing that he could be reproved for. He will openly have friends and openly have enemies so that all men may know which each are, one and the other, because to love or to hate privately is characteristic of poor men that dare not to take a hand openly. The brave will not believe what he takes in hand from the speech of the people, for he has more care of truth than of the opinion or the beliefs of the people. Therefore he is true in deed and word and has no will to lie, unless it be for mirth and play. He will have no company except with his friends, for to please all men is excessive servility and the brave will not endure that. But they that are of a low heart are lowly to all men and marvel of small things that they hear. The wise brave man marvels only at things of great value. The brave will have no remembrance of discomforts that he has suffered because he holds himself neither degraded by or underfoot of the discomforts that he has escaped. And because he took himself not to heaviness for the damages that befell him, but by virtue of strong heart he received them lightly, he may have no remembrance of them. Another manner the manly or the brave has is that he speaks and thinks little of what bears boredom. He also has no will to speak of himself or of another much; he has no concern that he should be praised or that others are blamed and therefore he praises neither himself nor others. Nor will he speak harm of his friends or of his enemies, but in all that he should do, he does it wisely without boasting and actively without cowardice. Another condition the manly or the brave has is that he never complains of deficiencies that he has had, of meat, drink, or of other necessary things. But he receives plenty and poverty of all things evenly so that no man may perceive, neither by word nor by semblance, that he has changed his heart from ease to discomfort, neither for scarcity nor for plenty. If it befalls that he has a need for any thing, he begs not gladly for another man's help unless there is great need to drive him. He does not reckon for much except for the common peace for the people, justice, right, and the honor of God above all things. The brave man desires more of honest things without winnings than dishonest things with great winnings. And therefore he desires more great lordship or little rent rather than a township of land or a great sum of cattle belonging to churls. It is characteristic to churls to praise much and to love great heaps of money of gold and silver because they have low and little hearts. However, a love of chivalry and lordship and a desire for strength, ability, and rightfulness without adornment belongs to noble people of high lineage and of great virtue. By nature the brave will be slow moving, for he seldom finds any thing for which he deigns to hasten. He should have a strong and great voice and speak truly for that is a sign of a strong and stable heart. Therefore women that are by nature feebler than men have small voices. Those men that chide hastily from rancor of heart have not their spirits in their power, but whosoever has the virtue of fortitude deigns not to chide and he has no need for haste in speaking for his spirit is not troubled by rancor.

Chapter 31: Here begins old stories to show the conditions and the properties of the brave or the manly

These old princes desire much to put their lives in balance for the common profit of the people and they were so brave that in such a point they feared not death. For as Valerius says and St. Augustine repeats in the book of *The City of God*, when Codrus, a former king of the city of Athens, going to a certain battle against his enemies, understood the answer from his gods that the side whose king or duke should be killed in battle would have the victory in battle. He unlaced his rich arms and his royal array, and clothed himself in poor array, and without any fear he went fully disarmed against the hosts of his enemies, and tarried them by contention, wherefore they instantly slew him. For he preferred to suffer death so that his men might have the victory, rather than live and see his men be overcome. The princes in old times were not covetous of gold or silver, and therefore they gave more gladly than received. Vegetius tells that a noble counselor of Rome that was called Fabricius was a wise and a worthy man that did not love to receive gifts.[44] He answered an ambassador from a distant, foreign country that offered to him a great sum of gold, saying, "Go to your country with your gold. I have no care to receive; rather it is preferable to me to command those that have the gold, than to have their goods." [45] Scipio, the noble duke of Rome, saw that Hannibal, the king of Carthage, the principal city of Africa, had besieged the city of Rome for a long time and had so greatly killed the Romans in one day that he filled three bushels with gold rings that were worn by the princes and the worthy men of the same Scipio. Then this Scipio, with his chivalry, passed across the sea and came to Carthage, laid siege to it and with great manhood he made strong and hard assaults. He killed the people by sword and through hunger, and tidings thereof he went to Rome. Hannibal abandoned the siege and went hastily to Carthage, entered with strength, and by great virtue restored the city. He made engines of war, gathered great hosts, defended the city, ordained his shield formations, and he gave stern battle, but at the last Scipio overcame him. Then Hannibal flew throughout all Africa into a stronghold of a castle. Scipio chased him as a greyhound does the fox. At the end, Hannibal drank poison of his own will and died so that he would not be taken or killed by the Romans. Then Scipio took all of Africa, made it subject to the Romans and was satisfied with a great tribute of gold and silver. He returned, whole and merry, to Rome and said to the Romans, "Fair sirs, I have conquered Africa for you and I have received nothing from the conquest except the name." As the time and the needs demanded, the princes in old time continued to have him sometimes as a lord for some time. This Valerius witnessed and tells that King Alexander led a great host in a time of very cold weather. At evening when he rested, he sat on one high seat by a fire; he looked about and saw an old knight quaking from cold. Instantly he descended from the seat, took the knight in his arms, and set him in the seat by the fire where he had sat. Therefore it was no marvel that men would so gladly serve such a lord that better loved his knight than his own dignity. Princes took great and high deeds on themselves in old times and small things they left to small men. Orosius, who well knew the stories, tells us examples of this. Cyrus, the king of Persia, strove to quickly conquer Babylon, the great strong city, but he was much hindered by a huge river running by the city walls. In a day when they would make an assault, a knight first set into the river with foolhardiness. The course of the river, which ran so strong and so stiff, took the knight and his horse, bore them down, and drowned them. Cyrus, the brave and mighty king, in great wrath said, "I shall take such cruel vengeance on this river that a woman with child will be able to pass through it without peril." Then he assembled workmen by the thousands that trenched and delved the ground and parted the river in three hundred and sixty parts, through which all men, small and large, might pass without any damage.

Then he took the city, destroyed it, and he cast down the walls to their foundations. It was not held to be prowess or chivalrous to assail an unwarned man and old men held it to be cowardly. Therefore Alexander, the son of King Priam of Troy was much to blame for killing Achilles, the worthy and able knight, in the temple of Apollo through deceit and treason. Holy Writ reproved Joab, prince of King David's host, because he had killed two princes by treason who were better that he was: Abner and Amasa. Therefore Solomon, King David's son, took vengeance thereof and killed him as the Book of Kings tells us. Old princes loved truth and verity more than opinion or falseness. Valerius gives us examples of that and says that in old times there were two friends, one was called Damon and the other, Pythias. Dionysius, the cruel tyrant and king of Sicily, took one of them and he would have him killed. He asked for a delay in his death to make his last testament and dispose of his goods. The tyrant granted it upon a covenant that he would put up a pledge for himself for a certain day and so he put his friend in for himself and went forth. Many days passed, the term neared and he came not. Every man held that the man who was bound was a fast fool and said, "You have acted in foolish haste by putting yourself as a hostage for your friend. He will not come again and you will die." He answered, "I know my friend well and he would not break a covenant at any time. I know well and I am certain of his return." When the term passed, his friend returned and he presented himself to the tyrant and said, "See me here, let my friend pass, for I have acquitted him." Dionysius remembered him with such great truth, friendship, and loyalty, and forgave his ill will and prayed them both to receive him as their fellow. Lying to please those great and small is contrary to the virtue of fortitude, and therefore the philosophers that were full of virtues say that it is better to suffer great distress than to obtain great wealth by lying. About deceiving to get great riches, Valerius also tells of Diogenes the philosopher. On a certain day he gathered cabbages for his food, and therefore a deceiver, Aristippus, said to Diogenes that was with Dionysius the tyrant, "Diogenes, you should have no need to eat cabbages if you would flatter King Dionysius." Diogenes answered, "And if you would eat such food, you should never need to flatter King Dionysius." None of the brave or manly are light of thought and they marvel not at what many poor men marvel at. Of this Valerius tells us that a lame man came to a certain battle and therefore some from the same battle scorned him. The lame man answered, "I am not maimed in hands nor in arms though I am lame. Therefore, I shall fight much better, for I have no hope to flee." He tells us of another, to whom his fellow said, "They have so many arrows in Persia that the sun grows all dark when they begin to shoot; it is better to flee than to assail so many people." The other answered as a brave man, "The many arrows that you speak of should please us much, for the weather is very hot and therefore we will fight much better under the shadow of the arrows." It does not suit him that is brave to think overly much about discomforts and adversities that are past for that will make him a coward. If King Alexander had had much thought for the tribulations and pains that he had suffered in Persia, he would never have been brave enough to enter into India. And if Scipio had regarded the damages of Rome too much, he would never have been brave enough to enter into Africa. We find written about the commendation of Scipio that as long as he had things to do, he thought that nothing was done. Julius Caesar gladly forgave the wrongs that were done to him and because of that, he got the lordship of all. The brave man has great sufferance, courtesy, stability, and truth, and therefore he does not regard praising or condemnation, for it is a great name, certain of good renown, which a man puts in another man's mouth to be praised. Indeed, by the speech of the people, a coward may be as brave as Hector of Troy. Nonetheless, as it is declared before in this book, a prince should desire and get good renown in foreign governance by obeisance to God, in wise governance of his speech in God's worship and by the profit of the people, and not in boasting as diverse men do, who give gifts to poets who praise most those people who give most. Every wise man, as a poet says, often should inquire how the people speak of him: "**Epius inquiras quid de te**

fama loquatur." That is to say, "Inquire often what thing it is that fame speaks about you." King Alexander was called, "Jupiter, the great god," by many a man that flattered him, but he knew well that they lied. And it happened in a time that he laid siege to a city where his army made an assault and the citizens defended themselves. Alexander was wounded in the thigh, but he would not depart from the army till the assault was fulfilled. Afterwards, he alighted from his horse and softly laughing said, "This wound shows well that I am not God, but a mortal man, for it grieves me sorely." Above all things in old times, princes loved the common good and the authorization of the people, and therefore they sought not riches or treasures for their own good, but for the common good. They sought neither dainty meats nor drink, but as little as they might for themselves and more for other men. Therefore, in my opinion, the great abstinence that our Irish enemies endure in meat and drink is much the reason they often have their purpose in war. For Valerius tells us about a governor of Rome that was called Marcus Curius; he was a great man of great knowledge, brave, and chivalrous, and he governed well the empire. Messengers came to him from a great city and they found him sitting by a fire upon a little chair, and eating from a wooden dish. They prayed to him if it was his pleasure to condescend and to receive a great sum of gold that they had brought him from their lords. This worthy lord began to laugh softly and answered, "Say you to your lords that sent you hither, that Marcus Curius had rather to command rich men than be rich; know that I shall not be corrupted by friendship, enmity, and neither by gold nor by silver." For as Valerius says, "Every good emperor loves better to be the poor in a rich empire, than be rich in a poor empire." St. Augustine says, "It is more to be lamented that the poverty of the empire of Rome is perished than its riches, for while the princes were poor, the people were rich, and when the princes were rich, the people were poor." Therefore, as Eutropius tells us in the stories of the Romans, Constance the emperor desired in all his time to make his people rich. Moreover, the same scholar tells us that better it is that riches are in the hands of many men than that they be enclosed in one place, for the richer the people are, the better they may defend them selves and therefore they have better character. Whosoever has little has less character and therefore if the prince impoverishes the people, he he may have less trust that the people will help him with good will. All the intent of good princes that ever existed has been to maintain the good of the common people, for in that deed they trusted the better to be like our Lord God, King of all Kings who governs all creatures after their degree. Therefore by great study the laws were established and maintained, merchandise used, diverse money contrived, and all that might be said that was good, all was provided for the common profit of the people and not to make the princes rich. All books that discuss empires or realms witness that. Cicero asks, "Should the son spare the father if he does anything against the common profit of the country?" Thereto, he answered himself, "That first the son shall pray the father that he withdraw himself, and if he will not, he shall threaten him, and afterwards, if need be, he shall accuse him. And he will prefer that his father be killed rather than the common good of the country and the peace be disturbed." These old princes were of great abstinence for at no time, he that is a glutton may be chivalrous. Of this we read in the noble history of the Romans that Caesar Augustus, lord of the entire world, was of great abstinence. He had no concern for delicate meats, but held himself content with common bread, great meats, and cheese of the oxen, for he would not give example of delights to chivalry. The princes in old times more desired glory, honor, and nobleness, than heaps of gold, silver, or precious stones. Examples of these are great in number, but to pass over this shortly, it suffices that in the stories of Romans we find written that one forcible king of great power besieged the city of Rome. Cruel assaults were made there and he had killed a large number of people, where he was feared and dreaded beyond measure. The senators of the city had to keep their counsel to the aforesaid people; they struggled much to contrive how they might overcome the tyrant and put away the siege that lasted for a long time. At that time in a pasture outside the city was a keeper of mules that the Romans called a mule driver[46]. Every day this mule driver beheld the hosts, he regarded their battle, he examined their arms, their countenances, and their leaving, early and late, and saw the king often going out of his tents privately to go to the siege; he knew him well by certain signs. One day the mule driver saw him going privately too far from his men and he hastened there quickly. This common man was strong in arms and he caught the king with great strength and trussed him on the front of his mule. He hastened fast on his way and never stopped until he came to the capital. There, as the senators were at counsel, he smote the door and asked entry. The porters held great indignation for him, left him there, up they went, and delivered his message. The senators were grieved to be troubled by a common man. At last one senator said, "We should not have contempt for the common man; we know not what tidings he has brought. Unless he had some great message, he would not be bold to come hither." And so by common assent, the common man had entry. A fair present he showed; he presented them the king of the barbarians to do their will with him. The barbarians had lost their king and it was no wonder that they were filled with terror. The Romans armed themselves fast and the barbarians were burdened. They sought their king, but he could not be found; they turned their backs, but it availed them little. The Romans pursued them; they smote, they hewed and they slew, and returned home with great victory. With great nobility they bore with them into the city, gold, silver, precious stones, and rich clothes; they slew the king, and so they made a good end of the war. After this the senators thought of what reward they should give the mule driver. They called him forth; they offered him gold, silver, and other advancements and asked him what he would be content with for his good service. He answered as a mighty and brave man that loved honor more than riches that soon would pass. "I have no care for gold or silver, but grant me one thing and that will suffice me. He said, "Make an image in brass of my likeness and of a crowned king overcome by me." They did so, and set the image in the street so that all the people that went there might have a remembrance of that victory. Therefore Aristotle says that, "Honor is the highest thing that a man may have in this world." It pertains to the brave to be slow of moving, but when he takes battle in hand, he is so fierce that he fears no man. In the stories of the Romans we read that Tiberius, the emperor of Rome, tarried in all his deeds, and without ripe counsel he did nothing that caused burdens, for too much hastiness is not prowess. This emperor scarcely ever changed any officers he had made except for overt falseness. One day one of his private men asked this emperor why he did this. He answered and said that he did so for the profit of the people and that he would show him by this example. There once was a man that had many wounds and lay naked in a wood; the flies that lay thickly on him sucked his blood. Another man passed by the way and had pity on him and drove away the flies. The wounded man said, "Alas, you have done me much harm and grief, for the flies that you have now chased away have eaten and are now full and these newly come will assail me much more smartly." So it is in the same manner of new officers in that they are like new hungry flies. He said, "Therefore, I will not easily change or remove officers, for all the time the latest are the most grievous as they are the most needy and least sparing of the people." To speak with good spirit and breath pertains to the brave, for that is a sign of hardiness of heart, great taking on, and stoutness. Speaking with little spirit signifies and shows a cowardly heart without boldness. Now I have told you the signs and properties of the brave of which Aristotle teaches.

Chapter 32: The pity and mercy that a prince should have

It is to be known that though humility is necessary to all men, it is namely necessary in princes. Therefore, it is to be known that God ordained Moses, the first prince of his people, who was brave and a very humble man, above all men that dwelled on earth. In the gospel of Matthew, it is written, "**Ecce rex tuus venit tibi mansuetus, et lex eius vocabitur lex clemencie.**" That is to say, "See your king comes to the humble, and his law is called the law of humility." The last *Book of Proverbs* says that Christian kings and the prelates of holy churches are anointed in signs of humility. Seneca says, "**Nullum ex omnibus clemencia magis quam regem aut principem decet.**" That is to say, "Humility makes no man of the people fair or seemly more than a king or a prince," for humility is the distinction and the difference between a king and a tyrant. And it is to be known that the virtue of humility keeps the mean between sparing and vengeance at times. For Seneca Says, "**Tam omnibus ignoscere crudelitas est, quam nulli, Medium tenere debemus.**" That is to say, "It is cruel to forgive all men, as well as no man; therfore we should hold the mean way." He that is a governer shall spare sometimes, and in other times he shall take vengeance. The virtue of temperance, namely in a prince, pertains to humility in taking vengeance for the wrongs that are done to himself. For just as it does not befall a mighty man to be liberal with another man's goods but to be liberal with his own, so is the Prince called humble, not in forgiving his people's lusts, but in his own not departing from the virtue of temperance. Therefore great honor, glory, and perpetual worship are for the prince, namely in redressing by the force of power and law the wrongs that are done to the common people and to his subjects, by enemies, thieves, and other extortionists. Seneca tells us one example why a prince should be patient and humble: the bee is an exceedingly wrathful beast and full of fight and they leave their stinger in the wound in vengeance, but the king of bees is without a stinger. This is a natural nobility of the unreasonable creature that gives an example to all princes and governors of the people. Another example I find written is of the lion; although a man has hurt him sorely and he that hurts him falls down to the earth and cries mercy to him, he wills the man no discomfort in anything. Therefore Julius Caesar forgave nothing easily except the wrongs that men did him and if any man slandered him, he never answered him or took vengeance on him. We read about this emperor that a man of evil will called him a 'tyrant', and he answered, "If I were a tyrant, you would say so no more." It was true, for he might have killed him. The emperor Theodosius made a statue and said, "If any man slander our names, we will it not that he be therefore punished, for if it comes from lightness, it is to be despised, and if it come from madness, a man should have pity there. And if it comes from malice, it is to be forgiven." Seneca, the good scholar, tells that the citizens of Athens sent messengers to King Phillip of Macedonia. When they had given their message the king said to them demurely, "Tell me what thing it is that I may do to please the lords that sent you to me?" They said to him, and especially one of them that was called Timocharis, "If you would hang yourself, it would greatly please them." When the kings' knights heard that, they would have him instantly hewn into small pieces had not the king defended him. He said, "Let no man be so brave as to do him any harm." Then said he to the messenger, "Go to your lords that sent you hither and say to them on my behalf that they are more proud and are less to be praised who send such a message than they that heard the message and took no vengeance." The wise poet Cato says, "**Vtilius regno, meritis adquirere amicos.**" That is to say, "A more profitable thing than a kingdom is to get friends by good deserving." However, Dermot MacMurrough did not do so. He was the Prince of Leinster, which is fifth part of Ireland. Richard Cambrensis, a great scholar who wrote the story of the conquest by King Henry the Second in Ireland, tells us that in the beginning of his reign this Dermot was an oppressor, an extortioner of virtuous men, and a cruel, intolerable tyrant upon the great lords of his land.[47] Another mischief befell him; he kidnapped, with her own assent, the wife of O'Rourke, the King of Meath, in the absence of her lord. And because of that, for the most part, witnessing all of the mischief by many old stories and also new, begun by women, this king O'Rourke, more for shame than for a highly grieved hurt, grew all venomously wrathful. Therefore he gathered many foreigners, that is to say, Rourke of Connaught, at that time King of Ireland, with his people and his own, in order to be avenged. Then the great lords of Leinster, seeing their prince put to mischief, and in every part besieged with enemies, repeated old wrongs that he had done them. They rose all at once with his enemies and so fortune and his people left him at once. Then this Prince Dermot, seeing himself besieged on every side without help and favor and greatly beset with enemies after many sore battles, flew over the sea into Normandy into the part of France where King Henry the Second aforesaid was, for the last remedy and he vehemently sought succor from him. The King nobly received him and Dermot told him about his governance. When the King had heard the cause of his comin, he received from him the bond of subjection and fealty. He took his letters of commendation whereby he brought the power of Englishmen, Normans, and Welshmen into Leinster, and with that and the other four parts of the land, this same King Henry, for the most part, conquered. Thus did this Prince Dermot forever encumber in oppression himself and all the other princes of his nation on land.[48] Therefore it is better to every prince to command his people with them willing him well rather than them willing him evil. Nero and Domitian, the Emperors of Rome, felt this and King Richard the Second and many more before and since felt it too. This scholar, Cambrensis, tells in the same story, "**Expedit subiectis principi cuilibet pocius amari quam timeri.**" That is to say, "It is profitable to every prince to be loved rather than to be feared" by his subjects, and it is profitable to be feared, so that love rather than correction strengthens fear." For whatever man is loved, it seems that he is feared, but the common people hate every extortioner, and he that is hated by the common people shall not be succored when he has most need as Dermot the Prince was. I find in a written sermon that an extortioner is worse than the Devil, for the Devil takes in prey and torments only cursed men and the extortioner robs and preys on good and true men. Therefore the Devil may justify himself in comparison to extortioners, for the Devil may say to God, "I have tormented only those men that you have hated, but this extortioner has tormented the men that you loved." And so, we may understand that an extortioner is the Devil's angel, for they are sent into this world to do here that thing that the Devil does in Hell, that is to say, to torment.

But for as much, gracious lord, as I have here and now touched upon the conquest of Ireland, I shall now declare to you, as I find in part in the written chronicles, many titles of our liege lord, the King of England, and his right to this land of Ireland against the erroneous opinions of the heinous Irishmen, saying that they have the better right.

Chapter 33: The King's titles to the land of Ireland according to the chronicles

At the beginning, before the coming of Irishmen into the land, they were dwelling on a side of Spain that is called Basque. Bayonne is the chief city and a part of Basco. At the Irishmen's coming into Ireland, King Gurgent, son of the noble King Belyng and the King of Britain, the greater, that is now called England, was lord of Bayonne as our king is now. Therefore they should be his men and Ireland his land.[49] The second title is this: at the same time that Irishmen came out of Basque, exiled in sixty ships, they met with King Gurgent up the sea at the Orkney islands, coming from Denmark with great victory.[50] Then their captains Eber and Eremon went to this king, and told him of the cause of their coming and prayed to him with great instance that he would grant that they might inhabit some land in the west. At last, the king, by advice of his counsel, granted them Ireland to inhabit and assigned them guides for the sea thither. Therefore they must have been our king's men.[51] The third title is, as I have declared before, that Dermot, the former Prince of Leinster in Normandy, became liegeman to King Henry the Second, conqueror of Ireland. Through King Henry, he brought the power of the aforesaid people into the land and married his eldest daughter Eva to Sir Richard Fitz Gilbert, Earl of Strigoil, at Waterford in Wales, and granted him the reversion of Leinster with Eva his daughter. After that the Earl granted Dublin to his King Henry with two districts next to Dublin and all the haven towns of Leinster to have the other's part in peace and the king's good lordship.[52] Therefore MacMurrough had the least right to have lordship of all the other Irish captains and our king especially had good right to Leinster. It is to be known that a district, in France and in Ireland, is a portion of ground that may contain a hundred villages. In England such a district is called a hundred or a weapontaille.[53] A weapontaille is the equivalent of saying 'a taking of weapons', for in old times in England, at the first coming of a new lord into a district, the tenants of the same district would deliver to their lord their weapons as their homage. The fourth title of right that our king has to Ireland is that seen in the year of our Lord 1162.[54] The aforesaid King Henry landed at Waterford and Dermot, King of Cork, went to the king there and of his own proper will became liege tributary for him and for his kingdom.[55] On this he made his oath and gave his hostages to the king. Then the king rode to Cashel and Duvenald, King of Limerick, came to him there and became liegeman, as did the King of Cork.[56] Then Donald, King of Ossory, and MacSaglin, King of Offelan, and all the princes in the south of Ireland as well went to King Henry and became his liegemen as was aforesaid.[57] Then King Henry went to Dublin, and O'Carroll, King of Uriel, O'Rourke, King of Meath, and Roderick, king of all Irishmen of the countryside and of Connacht came there with all the princes and the men of value of the land, except for the people of Ulster, and became lieges and subjects. They made tributaries by great oaths, their kingdoms and their lordships to the aforesaid King Henry, by their own good will as it well seems, for the chronicles make no mention of chivalry, nor war, being done by the king at the time that he was in Ireland. The fifth title is this: For as much as Ireland is an island, and it and all other Christian islands belong to the right of St. Peter and the Church of Rome, Pope Adrian granted the lordship of Ireland to the aforesaid King Henry to increase therein Christian faith and holiness. And to set the people of the land in the governance of good laws and virtues, and to eschew vices. Pope Alexander, his successor, confirmed this gift and grant of Pope Adrian. These titles of right obviously appeared by the same Papal Bulls, the copies of which have been made abundant. Vivian came later. He was a legate from the Pope to Ireland and he assembled at Dublin all the clergy of the land at a counsel where this legate declared and affirmed to the clergy the king's right to be good to Ireland. He also commanded, and denounced all the people of Ireland on the pain of being cursed, that no man should presume foolishly to depart from the allegiance and the faith of the King of England. The sixth title is that assembled at Armagh. By the same council, the clergy of all the land at the time of the conquest up to the coming of Englishmen, it was described and determined that because of the sin of the people of the land by the sentence of God, the mischief of the conquest had befallen them. The seventh title is because at the first coming and presence of King Richard II in Ireland, at the city of Dublin and other places in the land, O'Neill, captain of the Irishmen of Ulster, O'Brien of Thomond, O'Connor of Connacht, Arthur MacMurrough, captain of Irishmen in Leinster, and all the other great captains of the Irishmen of Ireland came to him there by their own goodwill and became liegemen to the same King Richard. They did homage to him, as for a liege, and for greater surety they bound themselves in great sums by diverse instruments to pay to the Pope's chamber to truly keep and hold their allegiance in the aforesaid form. Therefore, from the beginning to the end, good is our king's right to the lordship of Ireland. Therefore they should hold themselves quiet who say the contrary.

Chapter 34: Now here I make an end of the third cardinal virtue that is called in Latin, fortitude, in English, strength. To treat the fourth cardinal virtue that is in Latin called temporancia. It is my intent, God helping. Amen

Scholars call the fourth cardinal virtue temperance, by which a man holds and keeps moderation in eating, drinking, and does not overindulge, as sin in women. It keeps him from all excess in all his deeds and speech. Therefore Cicero says, "If you desire temperance put away every excess and restrain your desires. Regard how much nature asks and not how much covetousness desires."

If you hasten the virtue of temperance, you will be satisfied with yourself without desiring to have more. For he has enough who is satisfied with what he has, for he will not desire more. He that covets more than he has acknowledges that he does not have enough. And therefore on your covetousness, set the bridle; in eating and drinking be temperate. According to what nature asks, use moderation. Little is better than too much, but the mean of both surpasses in bounty. When you are among company, you will not eat or drink that thing which you have reproached. To the delights that are present now, you will not give over to them too much and you will not greatly desire those that are absent. See that you can live on little meat and drink. Drink not for delight, as does the glutton, but for needs that you have. Let hunger give the appetite, rather than the savor of the sauce. If you are tempered by the aforesaid virtue, you will shun foul things before they happen, for no man taken suddenly keeps himself well. Whosoever will not shun evil company will suddenly fall into foul things. Behold well all the movements of the body and heart, that there be no filth in them. Never be hardier to do amiss because you are alone, by yourself, and where no man can see you, for a man may be destroyed by evil deeds, though other men do not see him do them. You shall not fear any man more than yourself, for every man is absent to you sometimes, but you are present to yourself at all times. All that you do privately, God sees it openly. Foul and unclean words shall you shun, for it is not far from the heart that the mouth speaks, and what is in the mouth soon proceeds to the deed. With your accusations you will meddle evenly and moderately without the impairment of dignity. Play not too much or laugh too much, for Solomon says, "Laughter is always in the mouth of the fool." The fool enhances his voice when he laughs, but the wise man thinks and laughs softly. There is a time for laughing, a time for weeping, a time for speech, and a time for being still. It is to be known that in two causes man should not laugh in any way: in spite at another man or for the mischief, which has befallen another. Whosoever laughs when he should not is held dishonest and whosoever never laughs is overly aloof in company. Show your wit and grieve no man; when you will play, you need to keep away from villainy. You will laugh without grinning, speak without crying or noise making, go without sloth, and rest without dishonesty. Above all things you will shun and hate perfectly flattery in yourself and in others, for flattery destroys every virtue. The flatterer will say to you, "God be thanked that you do well. You are full of virtues and knowledge. You are rich, stable, strong, worthy, brave, seemly, fair of body, large of heart, well spending, a noble man and of great peerage, and well proved in deeds of arms. So help me God, in all this land there is none your peer." Whosoever believes or trusts such flattery, will fall into pride and over confidence. Where they take such things in hand, they will never bring it to a good end. Solomon says, "The flatterer beguiles his friend with his mouth." Therefore Cato says, **"Plus alijs de te, quam tu tibi credere noli."** That is to say, "Do not believe another man's words about you more than yourself." You will withstand a flatterer utterly so that he will be rebuked. You will do it for your own profit and his also, for you will not be deceived and he will not take part in deception. Receive warning and admonishing gladly and reproving without wrath or grudging. If a man reproves you rightfully, you ought to express thanks to him, and if he does it wrongfully, it may be that he believed that he did it rightfully. If it is that he reproves you wrongfully, tell him the truth kindly, for there is no man that does not make a mistake at some time. Solomon says, "A blessed answer abates anger and a hard and a thwarting word raises strife and madness. Reprove a wise man and he will love you; reprove a fool and he will hate you." Cato says:

Virtutem   primam   Puta   compescere   linguam.
Proximus   est   ille   deo   qui   scit   racione   tacere,

That is to say, "Believe that principal virtue is to constrain your tongue, for he is nigh to God that can be quiet by reason." Therefore has nature surrounded man's tongue with teeth and lips as two walls to signify that no word should pass out unless it was tried with reason. Nature has granted us two eyes and two ears, but only one tongue to show us that we should see and hear more than speak. Solomon says, "All that the fool thinks he speaks, but the wise man abides the proper hour to speak." On speaking, a poet suggests six points to behold and keep by these verses:

Si Sapiens fore vis, Sex serua que tibi mando:
Quid loqueris, et vbi, de quo, cui, quomodo, quando.

That is to say, "If you will be wise, keep six things which I command you: namely what is it that you speak, where and of whom, to whom, what manner, and in what time." Vices and evil stains you will shun and hate in yourself, but another man's vices you will not be busy to inquire into or spy upon, for by reason, such a man is to be hated. When you would reprove an ill doer you will not do it over sharply, but in a fair manner. Reproof was found for the amendment of him that is reproved, but when a man is overly reproved, he hates his reprover, and so he is impaired and not amended. Therefore says Solomon, whosoever blows the nose overly hard draws blood and therefore with kindness and fair cheer you should reprove and easily forgive the trespasses. When a man speaks with you, hear him fairly and whatever his answer will be gladly let him say it. If he has contempt for your answer, never be moved because of that; do not chide or tell him your indignation, for it is a great honor to a man to withdraw himself from chiding. By this aforesaid virtue of temperance, you will be loved by all people if they that are lower than you are not held not in contempt. Do honor and reverence to your sovereigns and due company to your fellows. Give reverence and honor to sovereigns, help and succor to subjects, company and gentleness to fellows, be kind to all men, and flatter no man. Have few confidential men, do right to all men, be slow to anger, be ready to give mercy, be steadfast in adversity, and be well advised and humble in prosperity.

Chapter 35: Thus much have I said of this virtue, temperance, for this time; now here I write old stories in commendation of the same virtue

Aristotle, Prince of Philosophers, says that to the virtue of temperance two things pertain that are to be known: abstinence of meat and drink and chastity of body. Therefore men keep old virtues by these two things. This appears by this story: often when Alexander the conqueror was in travail, he asked not for meat, but for bread only so that he might endure abstinence. A great scholar, Vegetius, tells us in his *Book of Chivalry* that it pertains to a good knight to love neither ease nor delights of body. Abstinence and moderation is as seemly to a knight as to a monk. Valerius tells us that women of Rome in old times drank no wine, for through gluttony and drunkenness men fall often into lechery, which is contrary to chastity and to chivalry. Therefore as Valerius tells us, Cornelius Scipio, when he was sent by the Romans into Spain to make it subject to Rome, he soon commanded that no bordello was to be found in their company and therefore two thousand women were driven away from the host. The wise prince knew well that love of women and burning in the filthiness of lechery softens a man's heart and makes him like a woman, so that he loses his strength, bravery, manhood, and chivalry. A distaff and some flax agree more with a lecher than a sword, a shield or a buckler. Therefore poets say in the fables that the well of Salinas makes men that bathe therein to change into women, in significance and in meaning. That men who bathe themselves in the well of lechery lose virtue and valor and they become faint and cowards and as feeble as women are. The same scholar Valerius tells us of a noble young man that was called Spurina that was so fair of face, of body and of features that all women were moved and tempted by his great beauty. This young man well perceived that, but he had no inclination for folly and therefore as much as he would not be suspect of folly or give occasion or cause of ill and sin, he wounded all his face, and made many scars therein. Therefore, the beauty went away and the sin ceased. The renowned scholar Vegetius tells us of King Alexander that after a great battle was done and great prayer was taken, a noble damsel of great beauty was presented to the King. But he that had given all to chivalry had no care for lechery and therefore he deigned not once to regard her, but sent her to the same prince that she was married to before. When this prince and his men saw this they praised much the virtue and the great loyalty of Alexander, and there they received him as king and lord. Such another tale Valerius tells us and says that at that time when Scipio had won and conquered Carthage, as is in this book written before among all the other hostages, a fair maid of great rank was presented to him. When this conqueror had understood that a gentleman of the country had betrothed her, he made them bring her father, her mother, and the gentleman that she was betrothed to before him. He said to them, "This gold that you have brought to me for this damsel's ransom, I give it and grant free marriage to her and this gentleman that has betrothed her." All men marveled at this great courtesy and they served more gladly this noble lord. By this virtue temperance, a man governs himself and with the virtue of justice, other men. But it is rather more profitable for a man to govern himself than other men.

Chapter 36: Here it is to be known of the temperate love that should be between a man and his wife, and how he should know her temperately

The love and the fear of almighty God, maker and former of all things, preferred first and above all things, twelve causes to induce a man to love his wife reasonably and temperately. The first cause is that the Holy Writ so bids: "**Viri diligite vxores vestras sicut et Christus dilexit ecclesiam et semet ipsum tradidit pro ea.**" That is to say, "O you men love your wives as Christ loves the holy Church and gave Himself for it." Therefore a man should love the bodily and spiritual health of his wife, because Christ died for the health of man's soul and the remission of his sins. Therefore a man should mercifully forgive his repentant wife her trespasses. Upon this matter St. Augustine said, "**Cur enim ad huc reputamus adulteros quos credimus penitencia esse sanatos.**" That is to say,

"Why should we now hold men adulterers whom we believe are made whole by repentance." The second cause that should induce a man to love his wife is that her body is the body of her spouse, and therefore he should love her body as his own body for the wife has no power over her own body. The third cause is that neither of them is sufficient to bring forth alone the fruit of generation. The fourth cause is that woman was formed of man's rib; God would not form woman of the slime as He did man, but from man's flesh and bone so that he should love her as himself. The Holy Writ says, "Whosoever loves his wife, loves himself." The fifth cause is that a man promises woman love when he sets the ring on her finger and kisses her at Mass in the presence of Christ's body. The sixth cause is that they are relatives both of man and woman, for the married love each other. Therefore it is a wonder that so many of them love others that they, themselves, would be in discord with, for often two realms are brought to one accord by one matrimony. The seventh cause is that a wife leaves her father and mother and all her kin and cleaves to her spouse, and therefore he does wrong unless he loves her. The eighth cause is that unless they both love each other, they will be in great discomfort, for as a man rests not well under a dropping house, especially in a cold time, so a man rests not with his wife if contention is between them. The philosopher said, "**Vxor est aut perpetuale refugium aut perhenne tormentum.**" That is to say, "A wife is a perpetual refuge or an everlasting torment." The ninth cause is that it is very pleasant to God that man love wedlock. For Solomon says, "My spirit is pleased in three things that are approved before God and man: that is to say the accord of brothers, the love of neighbors, and a man and his wife assenting together well." The tenth cause is that a wife is a solace to a man and God's gift, and therefore Solomon says, "**Ve soli.**" That is to say, "Woe to him that is alone." However, he is not alone that lives in chastity, as honest maidens and widows in the worship of God. But a fornicator is held alone which is cursed by God, for when he sees and desires a woman's flesh, he sees his discomfort rather than his consolation. He sees the sword with which the Devil cuts him and he departs from God. The eleventh cause is that a wife is like an ornament of a household. For Solomon says, **"Sicut sol oriens in mundo in altissimo dei, sic mulieris bone species in ornamentis domus eius, et mulier diligens corona est viro suo.**" That is to say, "As the sun rises in the world to the highest places of God, so is the beauty of the woman good among the ornaments of her house, and a loving woman is a crown to her spouse." Speaking of beauty Solomon says, **"Sapiens non corporis sed anime respisit decorem.**" That is to say, "A wise man beholds not the fairness of the body but of the soul." A fool is over taken in fleshly things. The twelfth cause is that the Sacrament of Matrimony is a dignity ordained by God and in Paradise before any sin was wrought. Therefore Christ in the Gospel says, **"Quod Deus coniunxit homo non separet.**" That is to say, "That thing which God has bound, let no man separate." A doctor tells of the love that a wife should have for her spouse: first every woman should love and fear her husband so highly that she should believe no man more fair, wise, or stronger than her husband, and even though any other man is more fair, wise, or stronger then he is, she should not believe that.

Chapter 37: The commendation for and of the works of matrimony

It is to be known that matrimony is to be commended for many causes and especially at this time for five: First, it is to be commended for the authority of almighty God, ordainer of matrimony, and for the honor of the place that it was made in. For as St. Benedict ordained the monks rule and as St. Augustine ordained the canon rule on earth, almighty God that may not err made the Sacrament of matrimony in Paradise. Therefore if he trespasses that breaks the rule of St. Benedict, he that breaks matrimony which God has made trespasses much more greatly. The second reason that matrimony is to be commended is for the oldness of it. This order is not newly made, but in oldness it passes all manner of orders on earth, for it was made before man ever sinned. The third reason is that, God, when the entire world was drowned during Noah's flood, saved only the order of matrimony. In Noah's ship, he and his wife, their three sons and their wives were saved, but all the lechers and concubines were drowned. The fourth reason is that Jesus Christ, his mother, St. Mary, and his disciples, by their bodies' presence-as St. John in his gospel tells-worshipped at the feast of wedlock. They were there eating and drinking, but lechers and concubines may not ever say that Christ or St. Mary, his mother, ate and drank in any of their houses, but rather the Devil did to whom they made a sacrifice of their bodies. The fifth reason is so that our Lord Jesus would be born of our lady, St. Mary, in matrimony. Moreover it is to be known that the work of matrimony may be used and done, as certain treatises of Wertius tells us, without any sin and merit in three cases. The first is when it is done for the cause of children to be conceived, and to the honor of God to be brought forth with other due circumstances according to reason. This is the principal cause and office of the work of matrimony. The second case is when the work is done as a remedy, that is to say, used to shun fornication. The third case is when debt is paid to the asker. Upon the same matter St. Augustine says thus, **"Redde debitum coniugale nullus est criminis. In hoc causu mouet Iusticia."** That is to say, "To pay wedlock's debt is no sin; rightfulness moves you in this cause." The fourth case is when a man asks his wife to make that work, so that she falls not in sin; as when a man knowing his wife is shamefast and would never ask for that debt and he fears her falling in sin.[58] In this case, pity moves. But truthfully if a man uses that work to fulfill his concupiscence there is either a venial or a deadly sin. It is a venial sin when concupiscence is so far subject to reason, that he would not know her unless she were his wife; it is a deadly sin when that concupiscence is so immoderate that he would know her regardless of whether she were his wife or not. Also it is to be known that a worthy scholar, John de Burgh, in a book which he made that is called in Latin, **pupilla occuli Sacerdotum,** tells that a man is not bound to pay his wife the debt of wedlock in a holy place because some men might say that the place is polluted. But if a man and his wife were violently enclosed in that place a long time, it would be lawful for them to do that deed. Also, at high feasts and on solemn days in times of fasting and processions, a man and his wife should not draw nigh together, for in such solemn times special honor is to be done to God. Therefore one should abstain from lawful things so that thing that is asked for may be gotten the more easily. Nonetheless, whosoever is asked, he owes it to pay, unless he may defer it wisely and without peril, but he shall not ask for it in the aforesaid times. Therefore whosoever asks that deed in those times sins not, but whosoever asks, stirred with concupiscence, but not for the contempt of the time or holy church counsel, sins venially. Also in the time that a woman is with child, if that deed is asked it ought to be paid if it can be done without peril to the child; also, it may be asked without incurring a deadly sin. Nonetheless if it should turn to the peril of the child, it should neither be asked for nor given. In that case, the best thing is that a man should treat his wife like his sister and does not do that carnal work.

Concerning the four cardinal virtues, by which a man guides himself rightfully in the way of good manners, were the many people gone out of the way regarding this time I have discussed. Now I will return to that place where I left off: *The Book of the Governance of Kings and Princes*, following in this same manner.

Chapter 38: The keeping of the body after the counsel of physicians[59]

Alexander, especially keep yourself from venom and poisons. Well we know that many kings and princes that might not have been overcome by armies with venom have lost their lives, by the hand of that man in whom they most trusted, and namely by women, for the love of women blinds the understanding of men and makes them trust too much in women. Therefore you should not trust in women before you have tested them, for as soon as you trust in a woman, your life is in her hands. Alexander, you should well remember that the former Queen of India sent you fair and great gifts, among which she sent you a very fair damsel with whose beauty you were soon caught. But I who was present there with you carefully, diligently, beheld that damsel, her countenance, and her reproachful look. I perceived that she had freckled eyes and that she fixed her sight on men faces without shame. By that I understood well that every man that touched her would soon be infected with venom, without hope of life, for she was nourished as a child with venom and therefore she was all venom. If I had not warned you thereof, at your first touching she would have destroyed you. Therefore you should have with you good leeches and physicians at all times. And you will not trust in one physician, for he might harm you privately and more easily if he is alone. But many physicians together would not consent so easily to misdoing, for every one of them will doubt the other. Therefore, considering the best physicians of science and wisdom of the best reputation, take what you need of medicine by their counsel.

Chapter 39: Astronomy is necessary to keep a man's body

As Galen the very wise physician says and Isidore the good scholar witnesses, a man may not perfectly know the science and craft of medicine unless he is an astronomer. Therefore you will do nothing, and namely that which pertains to the keeping of your body, without the counsel of astronomers. Believe not fools that say that no man may come to the science of the stars and the planets because they are so far from us. The old philosophers that have contrived that craft have made certain rules from the moving of the stars by often beholding, great vigilance, and by study. Moreover it is not for fools to believe that say that God has proved and ordained all that is to come, and therefore it is not profitable to know beforehand what is to come. By this reason, it is not worth the science and judgments of the stars. But I tell you, Alexander, that the glorious God has so established that the elements are governed by the stars and by the planets, that we obviously see. The sea moves and it withdraws according to the moving, growing, and decreasing of the moon that has mastery and lordship upon the water and upon all things that has the nature of water. Therefore, oysters and crabs, the brain and marrow of all beasts, increase and decrease after the moon. It is good to know beforehand things that are to come by reason of the stars and never later, for a man may better prepare himself against what is to come if he knows that a very cold wind and winter are to come and if he were wise, he would provide himself with warm clothes, wood, coal, and other things necessary by which he might escape the severity of the winter without impairment. In summer a man provides himself with cold meats, tempered drinks and cool houses. If a man knew dearth and great hunger were to come, the better would he provide himself with corn and other victuals. Therefore it well seems that those men are great fools that say that the science and judgment of stars is not profitable to know since that by them a man may better understand beforehand diverse perils and shun harm by knowledge and foresight. However, as much as the knowledge of a man is not sufficient without the help of God, the sovereign remedy against all harm and suffering is to pray to God almighty that He, for His great mercy, would turn harm into good, for His power is not made less, defiled, or disturbed by the virtues of the stars. Therefore, we should pray for His mercy by devotion, prayers, fasting, sacrifice, and by alms making so that He will have mercy for our sins. And if we so do, we may have hope that He will deliver us from the harm that we have well deserved.

Chapter 40: Here begins stories and examples to prove that prayer is a sovereign remedy in every tribulation

Whosoever will search the old stories since the world began will find manifested that nothing that man may do is of so great a virtue as prayer is. Abraham the noble patriarch, as the Book of Genesis says, prayed to God for Sarah, his wife, for she was barren and past the age of childbearing, but she conceived Isaac. This same Isaac had a barren wife called Rebecca; he prayed to God that He would give him offspring, and she conceived Jacob, the holy and noble patriarch. From these three descended Mary, the fully blessed virgin mother of our Lord Jesus Christ. In the time of Moses, the leader and governor of the people of Israel, we read that a people called the Amalekites fought against Israel. Moses would not enter into the battle, but reared his hands toward Heaven and prayed to God with a pure heart that He would help him. And it befell that while he had his hands upraised, Israel overcame their adversities, but when he lowered his hands, the Amalekites overcame Israel. Therefore two men supported the hands of Moses until the time that the Amalekites were overcome and killed. Therefore we understand that prayer better defends a man in battle than a shield or a buckler and it is better in battle than a sharp sword of steel. Joshua, the worthy and wise warrior in his great distress, overcame his enemies by prayer as we read in the Bible. When this Joshua, successor of Moses, had entered the Promised Land and took the city of Gibeon, and had gotten great goods and riches, five kings of the land stood against him: that is to say, the king of Lachish, the King of Jerusalem, The King of Hebron, the King of Jarmuth, and the King of Eglon with their hosts. Joshua went against them with his chivalry and prayed to God to be his help. God answered him, "Never fear them, I shall help you. No man will withstand you." Joshua assailed them bravely and God terrified them so much that they dared not defend themselves; instantly they turned their backs. The children of Israel chased them with great speed, hewed, and killed them, and as many as escaped the sword of Joshua, God cast them down with large hail stones that then fell through God's bidding (whom all things serve, as says the holy prophet David). Many more people were dead from the hail than by the sword. Joshua feared much that the day failed him such that he might be fully avenged, but by the great trust that he had in God, he commanded the sun and the moon that they should not move from that place, where they were at that hour and until the time that he was avenged on his enemies. God granted him that and the sun stood amidst the firmament for the space of one whole day, so that before or afterwards there was not so long a day. Scarcely any of the five hosts escaped and the five kings were taken and hanged. Ezekiel, the good king of Jerusalem defended himself better by prayer than by sword, for as the *Book of Kings* tells us, Sennacherib, King of Assyria, destroyed the cities of Judah and afterwards, besieged Jerusalem. Forasmuch as he had so great a power that he understood that no man might withstand it, he sent by three messengers to King Ezekiel saying that he was a fool if he thought he could defend himself against Sennacherib. None of the kings of the other lands could withstand him and Ezekiel should never trust in the help of his god, for no god, of all that were thereabout in all regions, could not defend their land against the Assyrians. This King Ezekiel trusted in God and clothed himself in a sack. He put himself to penance and prayers and he sent to Isaiah, the holy prophet, that he should pray for him and his realm. Both prayed to God that made Heaven and earth, in whose power all things were, that He would openly show to all nations that He alone was God almighty and that He would give mastery to whom He willed. Their prayer was not in vain, for in one night the angel of God came to the host of Assyrians and slew one hundred and eighty five thousand of them. When Sennacherib saw that it was no wonder that he no longer had the will to abide; he therefore hastened away until he came to the great city of Nineveh, but he could not hasten so much but mischance was at his back.[60] Both his sons killed him when he honored his god at his temple. It befell thereafter that Ezekiel grew sick nigh to death, and Isaiah the prophet came to him and said to him, "Our Lord says that you shall die and not live." The king was sorrowful; he turned toward the wall, wept tenderly, and he prayed for longer life. Isaiah went his way but it was not long after then that God said to him, "Turn again to Ezekiel, the leader of my people, and say to him on my behalf: I have heard your prayer and seen your tears, and I have healed and saved you. The third day you will go to the temple and I will grant you fifteen years more to live than you should have." Therefore it is to be understood that every man's life is marked by nature as far as how long he shall last and that term no man may pass. But by folly and evil keeping, he may shorten it. However,

God that is above all nature may fulfill both after His own will. Therefore Ezekiel lived much longer by the grace of God than by what nature granted him. Manasseh, the son of Ezekiel, was a very cruel tyrant. He slew Isaiah the prophet who healed his father and who saved the realm and the people. He made false prayers to false gods and honored them. He filled Jerusalem with innocent blood, believed dreams and sorcery, and he gave himself to every evil craft. Shortly to say, he surpassed in wickedness not only the kings of Judah and Israel that were before him and after, but with that he surpassed in wickedness and malice all the pagans and unbelieving men, overturned all the temples, and made it all as he was himself. Therefore God, that may not suffer wickedness to always endure, sent a tyrant to chastise that other. For the princes of Assyria came with very great power and conquered the city of Jerusalem; they took Manasseh the King, led him in chains to the city of Babylon, and set him in prison. Then he thought of the great noble that he had demeaned in Jerusalem, there as he was crowned king, and he became mournful and sorrowful, he reflected greatly that he had grieved God so much, and he cried mercy for his sins. Manasseh entirely prayed that He would deliver him and promised to make amends if he might come again to his realm. In this way, he knew God again in anguish and in discomfort, which he had forgotten when he was in his goodness and very well at ease. God, who is full of mercy and who refuses no man, no matter how much he had angered Him if he will repent of his misdeeds and cry mercy from Him with a perfect heart, forgave Manasseh his horrible sins and brought him into Jerusalem again. He gave him the kingship and he kept the covenant. Manasseh became a good man, destroyed the alters and oratories which he had edified to do his sacrifice to false gods, served God all his life well and truly, and died after he had reigned fifty-five years.

Chapter 41: God has no contempt for the prayers of pagans

Concerning the great virtue of prayer that God shows to those who keep the law of God and who believe and know the right, although some of them were wicked until this time I have told you shortly. But now I will tell of greater marvels and I shall show you that God has no contempt for the prayers of pagans if they pray to him with a good heart. God sent the prophet Jonah to the great city of Nineveh, which was a three-day journey. He said, "Go to the city of Nineveh and say to it, that before these forty days pass, the city shall be destroyed." Jonah entered the city in one day's journey and preached to those of the city that were pagan all that God had said to him. They soon believed the word of God and were sorrowful and repentant of their sins and they fasted and clothed themselves in sacks, small and large. From this came tidings to the king of the city and he soon arose from his royal throne, put off from him his clothes, clothed himself in sack, sat in the ashes, and made a cry throughout all the city that men and beasts should fast, be clothed in sacks, and that every man should turn from his bad life and his wickedness. When God saw this, he changed his sentence and forgave them their sins, for they cried for mercy with pure hearts, although they were pagans. I shall tell you another marvelous example to prove the same. When Alexander had conquered Egypt, Persia, and Mede, he passed towards the Caspian Mountains. Between them dwelled the ten tribes of the people of Israel from the time of Salmanasar, the great king of the Assyrians, who had destroyed all the land of Samaria, taken the children of Israel, and made this land his as the *Book of Kings* tells us. It was provided and ordained by the Assyrians that the children of Israel were not brave enough to pass the aforesaid mountains without permission. Therefore when King Alexander came to the mountains, these children of Israel asked for permission to go out if it pleased the king, for he was king at that time of that land. Then the king inquired as to why they were led out of their land and he understood from those who knew the truth that they had not held to the law of God of Heaven, which they had received from Moses, and that they had worshipped false gods that were made by men's hands, for which they were led into slavery. Therefore the prophets of God prophesized of their slavery and said that they should not come again from that exile. When Alexander had understood that he answered that he would not give them permission to go out, but he would enclose them more securely. Then he began to stop the passes between the mountains, but after he perceived that the work of man would not suffice for that, he prayed to God that He would fulfill that work. Soon the mountains joined themselves together so steadfastly that none of them might leave by any device nor other men enter to them by any craft. Therefore it is no marvel if God does much for the orison and prayer of a good Christian man that leads a good life when he did so much for pagans and sinners.

Chapter 42: Now gracious lord, to your excellence, I write here diverse right, good, and necessary notable instances of the virtue of prayer, first in Latin and then in English according to diverse, most authentic authorities of Holy Writ

First, it is to know that prayer sometimes is said to be a good work, on which matter St. Paul says, "**Sine intermissione orate.**" That is to say, "Pray without ceasing." Upon this matter the gloss says, "**Semper orrat qui bene agit.**" That is to say, "He prays at all times who does well at all times." Also the rightful man never ceases to pray, unless he ceases to be a rightful man. Whosoever will first pray must consider his own faults, amend them, and then pray. For Solomon says in the Third Book of Kings, "**Templo edificato si quis cognouerit plagam cordis sui, et extendit manus suas in domo hac, tu exaudies illum in celo.**" That is to say, "Now that the temple is built, whosoever will know the wound of his heart and put up his hands in this house, you will hear him in heaven." Also the gloss says, "**Oracio est cultus deo debitus, que comprehendit fidem, spem, et caritatem.**" That is to say, "Prayer is a worship owed to God that comprehends faith, hope, and charity." Therefore St. Augustine says, "**In fide, spe, et charitate**

continuato desiderio semper oremus." That is to say, "We pray at all times with faith, hope, and charity in continual desire." St. Matthew says, "**Et nune clamemus in celum**" ("Now we cry to Heaven"). St. Luke says, "**Petite et dabitur wobis, querite et invenietis, pulsate et apperietur vobis**" ("Ask and it will be given to you. Seek and you will find. Knock and it will be opened to you"). Upon this text, St. Augustine says thus, "**Non tantum hortaretur deus vt peteremus, nisi dare vellet, erubescat humana pigricia, plus wlt ille dare, quam nos accipere; plus wlt ille misereri, quam nos a miseria liberari**" (God would not so much admonish that we should ask, but if He would give. Man's laziness increases shame quickly, for He will give more than we will take and He will have more mercy than we desire to be delivered of discomfort). St. James says, "**Si quis indiget sapiencia postulet eam a deo, et dabitur ei**" ("Whosoever needs wisdom, ask God for it and it shall be given to him"). Isidore says, "**Qui vult oracionem suam volare ad dominum, faciat illi duas alas, Ieiunium et elemosinam**" ("Whosoever will fly his prayer to God, make for it two wings: fasting and almsgiving"). It is to be known that prayer helps sickness of the body, as Solomon says, "**Fili in tua paupertate ne despicias te ipsum, set ora dominum et ipse curabit te**" ("O son in your sickness despise not yourself, but pray to our Lord and He shall cure you"). St. James says, "**Oracio fidei sanabit infyrmum**" ("The prayer of faith will heal the sick man"). Also prayer lengthens a man's life as it did the aforesaid King Ezekiel. Also prayer delivers a man from shame and peril of death as it did the good holy wife, Susannah. Prayer also delivers a man from the power of wicked princes, as it did Baruch and many others; from prison as it did St. Peter; and from wicked serpents as it did St. Margaret, St. George and the king's daughter. Also by St. Patrick's prayer Ireland was delivered and cleansed of all venomous beasts. Also by prayer, the holy prophet Jonah was delivered out of the whale's belly. St. Jerome says, "**Ieiunio sanantur pestes corporis, oracione pestes mentis**" ("With fasting the sickness of body is saved and with prayer, the sickness of the soul"). Also prayer overcomes and has victory in bodily battle. The *Book of Exodus* proves this, saying, "**Cum leuaret manus Moyses, vincebat Israel**" ("When Moses upraised his hands, Israel overcame"). The *Book of Judith* speaks of this, "**Memores estote Moysi serui Dei, qui Amalech non ferro pugnando sed precibus sanctis deiecit**" ("Be you mindful of Moses, the servant of God, who cast down Amalek, fighting not with ire but with holy prayer"). Upon this text says the gloss, "**Plus vnus sanctus proficit orando, quam innumeri peccatores preliando. Oracio sancti celum penetrat quomodo in terris hostes non vincat. Plus vetula vna adquirit de celo vna hora orando quam mille milites armati adquirant de terra longo tempore preliando.**" ("One holy man profits more in praying than numerous sinners in battling. The prayer of the holy man penetrates Heaven. Why should it not then overcome enemies? One old woman gets more from Heaven in one hour of praying than a thousand armed knights get inland while battling for a long time"). To prove that prayer helps greatly against the malice of enemies, I have written diverse good old examples in this book above. Even so, insofar as good new examples should not be forgotten, for the learning of those that are to come, I write about one of them here now.

Chapter 43: Right, good, diverse, and necessary noble instances for the virtue of prayer

In the year 1422 after the incarnation of our Lord Jesus Christ, all the clergy of Dublin considered the great mischief of the Irish enemies and rebels in the land who were in the act of defiling. These are the ones to know: the Briens of Thomond, the Burkes of Connacht and Munster, the Murphys of Leix, the MacMahons from the country of Uriel (burning it more deeply than ever before), and O'Neill of Clandeboy, Cragfergus and Ulster (burning and wasting at his own will). Twice every week and in an open procession, this clergy prayed to God for the good success of the aforesaid, our King Henry, then in France, and for the aforesaid earl, his lieutenant of Ireland, against the malice of the aforesaid enemies. This earl, through the grace of God and the aforesaid devout prayers, was with the host of Dublin, burned and destroyed all of the most inland pastures, places, and towns of Leix with much of their props and their grains, then and after. Soon afterwards he rebuked the aforesaid Briens, Burkes, and diverse others and reformed them to peace. After that, this earl and the same host of Dublin, with his company and many more, rode by Dundalk and Magennis country and through O'Haggerty's country into the most inward strengths of MacMahons country and therein he was lodged three nights. This earl broke, burned to the ground, and destroyed MacMahons' new strong castle, his towns, his fair towers, and his strong places, and he killed many of his people and the entire remnant were discomfited.[61] With his people on the fourth day, the earl went safely throughout the central stronghold of Manus McMahon's country without any fight or shot from any enemy in the town of Arthyrde. The next week after that, at all the strongest passes, this earl cut, burned, and destroyed this same Manus' country with its grain; no enemy seen there, as ever before that were prone to fight with Englishmen, could withstand the assault. After this and without delay, this earl rode into O'Neill of Clandeboy's country with his retinue. There, God sent him a gracious exploit and saved him from treason. This O'Neill of Clandeboy, with all the greatest enemies of Ulster, was reformed to peace. Then this earl, with all his retinue, safely repaired to the town of Drogheda and there these MacMahons, with diverse other enemies, sued for peace with compensation. The aforesaid expedition, journey, and hard work were all done and fulfilled in the space of little more than three months, by the grace of God, in whom is all-and by devout prayer, the king lost no liegeman. Also a little before the aforesaid expedition, this earl rode for forty days through Thomond, that is the most inward strength of the Irish in all the land, and burned it. Many men therein he killed, and from thence repaired without loss to reckon; and he committed many other acts of prowess in that year that he was lieutenant. This noble earl should not have pride due to his acts of prowess for four reasons.[62] The first reason is that, as Matthew Paris says, the first part of the profit of every good work is glory pertaining to our Lord God. And therefore the apostle says, "Honor and glory are only in you, God." The second reason is that the second part of the profit of every good work is a good example for our neighbor. Therefore Christ, in the Gospel of Matthew, says, "Light your light before men so that they see your good works better." The third reason is that the third part of the profit of a good work is a meed or a reward for him that does good works. Therefore he that seeks his own glory for the good works that he does defrauds God of His part of the profit. Therefore Bernard says upon this verse, "**Scuto circundabit te veritas eius, etc**:" That vainglory is an arrow of the Devil that flies easily into your life and that is to be feared, but it makes a very heavy and sore wound.[63] The fourth reason why this noble earl should not have pride for this aforesaid prowess is the little thanks that he received from them who should have rewarded and commended him best. Therefore this noble earl may say what the apostle said unto Timothy. He says, "Know that in the last days there will be perilous times and men will be self-loving, covetous, proud, haughty, blasphemous, disobedient, and unkind withal." Seneca speaks of unkindness and says, "He is an unkind man that denies one to receive a good deed. He is unkind that feigns. He is unkind that does not reward or commend good deeds, but reports ill deeds. He is the most unkind of all that forgets good deeds." But yet, were it so that no man would reward or thank another for doing good deeds, nevertheless a man should not cease in any time to do all the good that he can. The prophet bids, "Decline harm and do good." And also our Lord God suffered no ill deed to be left unpunished or any good deed unrewarded.

As it was previously written, I declared how prayer helps much against bodily enemies: Now it is to be known that prayer helps much against spiritual enemies

The great scholar Isidore says, "**Hoc est remedium eius qui viciorum temtamentis exestuat, vt quociens quolibet tangitur vicio, tociens se ad oracionem subdat, quia frequens oracio viciorum impugnacionem extinguit.**" That is to say, "This is the remedy for him that burns with the temptation of vices: as often as he is touched with any vice, that often should he put himself to prayer, for often prayer quenches the pricking of vices." Also prayer puts away devils, as Matthew in the gospel says, "**Hoc genus demoniorum non eicitur, nisi per oracionem et Ieiunium**"("This kind of devils is not put out except by prayer and fasting"). Also prayer torments the Devil and it eases a man towards the love of God, it puts away sin, and it comforts a man in tribulation. Also prayer is good for tranquility and peace and I shall find many authorities for this in Holy Writ. St. Gregory says, "**Magna virtus oracionis que, effusa in terra, in cel operatur**" ("Much is the virtue of prayer which spoken aloud on earth, works in Heaven"). The gloss says, "**Oracio velut quoddam scutum ab ira dei protegit.**" That is to say, "Prayer defends the wrath of God as a shield." However, whosoever wills that his prayer to be heard by God, he must keep his commandments. Isidore says, "**Qui a preceptis dei auertitur manus, quod in oracione postulat non meretur, nec impetrat ab illo domino bonum quod poscitur, cuius legi non obedit: et si id quod Deus precepit facimus, id quod petimus sine dubio optinemus.**" That is to say, "He that is turned from the commandments of God deserves nothing which he asks in prayer; neither does he get from that Lord, whose law he does not obey, the good that he asks. If we do what God commands, we will get without doubt that thing for which we ask." Therefore St. Augustine says, "**Citius exaudytur vna obediens oracio quam decem milia contemptorum.**" That is to say, "Sooner is one prayer of the obedient graciously heard, than ten thousand of a rebel or an evil liver." In time of prayer a man should only think of God. Therefore Isidore says, "**Pura est oracio quam in suo tempore seculi non interueniunt cure. Longe autem a Deo est animus, qui oracionibus cogitacionibus seculi fuerit occupatus.**" That is to say, "That prayer is clean, with which, in its time, the cares of the world are not intermingled; that soul is far from God whose prayers are occupied with the occupations of the world." Therefore our prayer should be said having our hearts wholly in God, for the holy abbot Achon, says, "**Diabolus enim nullum opus tantum conatur interumpere quantum oracionem deuotam.**" That is to say, "For the Devil, no work is too busy to obstruct or to disturb as devout prayer is." Also we should pray to God having hope without any doubt, for St. Bernard says, "**Indignus celesti benedictione esse conuincitur, qui deum querit dubio affectu.**" That is to say, "He is convicted to be unworthy of the blessing of God that asks God with a doubtful will." Also it is to be known that we should pray in every place for in every place are perils and in every place we need the help of God. But Isidore says, "**Specialiter locus ydoneus orandi est secretus.**" That isto say, "A private place is an especially suitable place for praying." Also it is to be known that in prayer, the bliss of the kingdom of Heaven and the rightfulness of the kingdom should be asked for, especially at the beginning. St. Matthew says of this, "**Primum querite regnum Dei, et iusticiam eius, et hec omnia adicientur vobis.**" That is to say, "First ask for the Kingdom of Heaven and the rightfulness of it and all these will be given to you." However, God bids us that we should not ask first for temporal things, for temporal things belong to those men who have the rightfulness of the heavenly kingdom.

Chapter 44: The virtue of justice or rightfulness

The virtue of justice has been largely spoken about before in this book, but for as much as Aristotle's book makes mention of justice, I shall write to your nobleness here, the best words that are written therein. Justice is a virtue that is to be praised much for it is proper to the glorious God. Therefore the princes and lords who govern their subjects by justice, advance their needs, and defend their bodies and possessions are, like God, the sovereign governors. God governs the entire world by knowledge and justice. Contrary to these two virtues are folly and wrong. Therefore justice of a king or a governor is more profitable to subjects than plenty of riches and a rightful lord is better than seasonable rain. It is to be known that it was found written on one stone in the language of Chaldee, that a king and understanding are two brothers of which both have need of the other and that one does not suffice without the other. Justice, with rightfulness, is divided into two manners. One manner is when the judge does right to all men, large and small, according to the law; the other manner is when the judge stays rightful, as he is to God, and that he keeps himself from sins, which are against the law of God. Every good judge ought to have both of these things. By justice is the entire world governed; the world is like a garden of God and the walls that surround it are rightfulness. The rightful judge is as a lord surrounded with law and the law is a rod by which a king governs the realm. The king is an irresistible force that is defended by his barons and the barons are as soldiers sustained by money; money is fortune gathered from subjects. By justice, subjects are governed as servants and justice is the health of subjects.

Chapter 45: The governance of man through the five senses

God formed man and made him above the beasts; He gave man his commandments and promised him rewards after his deserving. He gave the body as a city to govern, placed therein understanding as a king, and set it in the highest place of man, that is, the head, and established for him five messengers to fetch and present all that is necessary to him. Those are the five senses, of which every one of them has his proper domain and each are set in certain places: in the eyes, in the nostrils, in the tongue, in the hands, and in the ears. By the eyes we know nine things that are to be known: light, darkness, color, body, shape, things near and afar, moving, and resting. By the ears we have knowledge of sound that is in two manners: sound which is called the voice of man or of beasts, as the speech of man, the neighing of horses, and the singing of birds. Another species of sense is called the sound of things that are not alive, such as the sound of water, the breaking of trees, thunder, harping and sounds of other instruments. By the nostrils we have knowledge of odors and stenches. By the tongue we feel the diversity of tastes: sweetness and bitterness, saltiness and sourness, and other tastes. Touch is a common sense spread throughout the body, but it shows him most by hands than any other limb of the body; by that sense we know hot, cold, dry, moist, and other such things.[64] All that these five senses receive are of those things that are without. They present to the imagination and moreover, they present to the understanding, which has to judge all things.

Chapter 46: The manner of properties for counselors

As the five senses are like five messengers, who serve the understanding, so Alexander, ought you to have five messengers and five counselors; and every one of them will be separate, for in that way will they be the most profitable to you. Keep your secrets to yourself and tell not what you have at heart to them. Take heed that they do not perceive that you have heed of their counsel, for then they would despise you. Therefore you should first assay their will and their knowledge so that you may better advise yourself to be well said and done. Therefore Hermogenes the philosopher says that the judgment of that man from whom counsel is asked is more be to praised than the judgment of that man that asks counsel even if he speaks better and wiser, for he that hears the reasons of many men may say the good easier than he that first speaks. When you have assembled your counselors to give any counsel, you will not meddle and give strange counsel so that they won't be disturbed. After you hear what they will say, and if they answer soon and in accord, you will then speak against them and, by some reason, you will show the contrary of that which they have said to make them think and cause them to be advised more thoroughly. When they have all counseled and their reasons are shown, you will not show what thing you most incline towards until the time comes for that deed and proof. You will subtly and quickly consider which of them gives the best counsel to you and what pertains most to the most profitable prosperity of your governance. Do not put that one higher than the others, neither in words nor in gifts nor by degrees of dignity, for from that often comes destruction in realms. You will do no great thing without counsel, for the philosopher says, that counsel is the highest of things which are to come, and that the knowledge and wisdom of the wise king is increased by counsel of good counselors, as the sea is increased by the receipt of fresh water and rivers. You may conquer by wisdom of good counsel much more than you can purchase by might of men of arms No harm may come from counsel, for if a man gives good counsel you may pursue it; and if it is unprofitable, you may shun it. I give you very good counsel that you not make only one man the keeper of your realm when you go into another place, for through his wicked counsel might the baronage be corrupted against you. One other counsel I give you is that you never spare your deadly enemy, but every time that you may, show your victory over him and keep yourself so that at no time he has power over you, for in no manner shall you trust him.

Chapter 47: How you will assay your counselors

One thing by which you may assay your counselors is that you will make them understand that you have need of money. If they say to you that it is good that you take from your treasure, know that they esteem you little. If they say to you that you should take greatly from the money of your subjects, know that they hate you beyond measure for that is but a corruption of your realm. If they say to you, "All that we have, we have purchased it by your grace in your lordship," they are to be praised and are worthy to commend as they, which desire the honor of their lord as their own. There is another manner in which you may assay your counselors. In the case that they gladly receive gifts and eagerly gather treasure to themselves, never trust to such, for they serve you to purchase gold and their greed never will end, for the more that money grows, the more greed increases. Ever such may be easily corrupted and by chance brought to that state that they would will your death by the enticement of those who would harm you and give him greatly for the harm. Therefore it is good that they be not far from your presence and command them that they have not acquaintance or familiarity with any other king or prince, and that they send no letters to them or receive gifts from them. If you perceive such things, address it in haste for men's hearts are very changeable and easily inclined to promises. He is the most profitable of your counselors and most worthy to be loved, who loves your life and is obedient to the death. He that most demeans your subjects to your love and he that abandons himself and his goods at your will, and he that has those virtues and the manners hereafter I shall tell of him.

Chapter 48: The signs and conditions that a good counselor and a friend should have[65]

At the beginning, your counselor and your friend should have perfection of limbs well enough to fulfill all the things for which he is chosen. Also, he should have good understanding and good will to understand what a man says to him. It is suitable that he should be of mind good enough to remember that which he has understood, so that he does not forget, that he be perceptive about which things bear command and which don't, and that he be courteous, well-spoken, and eloquent without talkativeness. He should be knowledgeable in diverse sciences. He should be truthful in word and in deed, hate lying, and love truth above all things. He should be gentle, kind, and conciliatory. He should shun gluttony, drunkenness and every excess of eating and drinking, lechery, foolish movements, and foul delights. Above all things he should be brave, stable of purpose, and love honor and highness; he should despise gold, silver, and other earthly things. He should think much of nothing, except dignity, honors, and lordships. He should love and hold in charity good and rightful men, hate wrongs, give each man his own, help those that have need, and when he would do justice, he should not make distinctions between people because God made all men alike. He should be of great perseverance in purpose and in deeds that he would do, pursuing and fulfilling them without fear and cowardice. He should know about the expenditures of the realm. He should not be of easy appearance so that he comes not into the contempt of the people. Nevertheless he should answer the people courteously and his court should be open to all those that come thither. Also, he should eagerly inquire and examine all manners of tidings. He should comfort the subjects, amend their deeds, and console them in adversities and in times suffer their ignorance and their simplicity.

Chapter 49: It is to be known how a man has all conditions of beasts

Know Alexander that the glorious God made no bodily creature wiser than man and that a man may not find any custom in any beast that is not in a man. A man is as brave as a lion, cowardly as a hare, greedy as a dog, brave and fierce as a hart, compassionate as a turtle dove, malicious as a lioness, secret and tame as a dove, deceptive and treacherous as a fox, simple and blissful as a lamb, swift and nimble as a kid, tyrannous and slow as a bear, precious and dear as an elephant, of little worth and as dull as an ass, profitable as a bee, libertine and dissolute as a goose, undaunted as a bull, reasonable as an angel, lecherous as a swine, malicious as a toad, profitable as a horse, and noxious as a mouse. Shortly to say, there is no creature in the world of which a man does not have some of its properties; and therefore a man is called the little world.

Chapter 50: Notaries

Alexander, it behooves you to choose wise men of perfect eloquence and of good mind to write your secrets and private works, for that is a sign of a great lord and it is a strong argument to show the highness of your might and the subtlety of your knowledge. For the sign and understanding of a word is as one's spirit, and the words are spoken as a body, but the writing is as a covering of the word. Before all things he needs to be of good faith, know your will in all things, and that he desire your profit and honor before all things. He should be courteous and perceptive in his deeds and allow no man to enter within sight of your private writings. If you find such as him, pay him well for his service so that he holds himself compensated to do you better.[66]

Chapter 51: Messengers and how they should be

Know, Alexander, that the messenger shows the knowledge of the man that sends him and he that is his eye in that which he can not see, his ears in that which he can not hear, and his tongue in his absence. Therefore you need to choose the most worthy, wise, worshipful, and commendable, and hate every manner of filth and villainy, that are in your presence. If he does not have all these conditions, for it is hard to find such, at the least he should be secretive and true; he should diminish nothing, nor make less or more the messages or needs which he is sent for, he should keep your commandments, and he take heed to the answers that he hears so that he can say them again when he comes. If such a man may not be found, at least he should be a true bearer of letters that are sent and be brought back again. Of these three messengers the first is the most profitable, the second most certain, and the third least perilous. If you perceive that any of those messengers are tempted to gather money or to purchase from the places that he is sent to, refuse him at all points for he goes not for your profit. Send not a drunken messenger, for the people of Persia are prone to force messengers to drink good wine and if the messenger becomes drunk, they know by that that their lord is not wise. You will not make the greatest of your private counselors your messenger and he shall not be far from your presence, for that would be an impairment to your realm. Often you should test all your messengers for what knowledge, what governance, and what manner they have. You will reward them well that are good and true. If any of them are found fully prepared to receive gifts, be greedy, and desirous to discover your secrets, he should be punished after his desert, but the measure of the punishment I will not tell you.

Chapter 52: How subjects are the treasures of princes and like a garden of diverse trees grown therein

Know well that your subjects are your treasures by which your realm is confirmed. You shall learn well that your subjects are like a garden in which are diverse manners of trees, and you will not hold them as land bearing thorns without fruit. While your subjects remain in good condition, they will remain the defense of your realm and of your power, therefore, you should govern them well, defend them from wrongs, and help them in all their needs. Therefore you need to have a constable that will not be a destroyer of your trees, but a keeper and a saver. He should be of very good manners and virtues, wise, and patient. Make of one man a sovereign, for if there were many, one should have envy for that other so that he should try to surpass him and from him much harm might come. Some manners of bailiffs show themselves true and beneficial to the king, but nevertheless they destroy the people; and each of them thinks in diverse ways about how he may long abide in his office. There are some

Chapter 53: Barons and what they serve in the realm

The barons increase and multiply the realm. The country is honored and the empire is ordained in degrees by them and, therefore, you should put them in certain dignities and power. You may ordain them very well in fours if you will, for four differences are chosen that are to be known: before, behind, on the right side, and on the left side, as there are four parts of the world: east, west, north and south. Therefore you may ordain that in every fourth part of your realm is one governor. If you see that they are more numerous, see that there are ten, for ten is a perfect number and it contains in itself four numbers that are to be known: one, two, three and four, which if they are added, makes ten. Therefore I should ordain that every governor has ten vicars in his host and in his turn, every vicar has ten leaders, every leader has ten captains, and every captain has ten men. All these assembled make a hundred thousand fighting men. When you have need for the service of ten thousand men, name a governor and he will serve ten vicars. With every vicar will come with ten leaders, with every leader will come with ten captains, and with every captain there will be ten men. That will make a number of ten thousand fighting men. So may you understand more or less. By this ordinance and this account, you may be relieved of costs and you will achieve your purpose and you will lighten the travails of your baronage; take heed that all your captains are chosen men. It is very necessary for barons to have wise and discrete notaries that are true and well proved in chivalry that can discern those which are worthy to bear arms. You shall honor all knights, holding none in contempt, neither rich nor poor. You should have with you the instruments that you decide to be made, for it will benefit you much to assemble many people

Chapter 54: A king should not enter into battle in his own proper person

You shall not do battle in your proper person where you may shun it. At all times keep yourself with the best and the greatest of your power. Promise honors and rewards to knights and keep your promises. When you must go with the armies, never go disarmed in case of sudden chances. Have good guards and good spies and good guarding, especially at night. When you are about to stop your army and pitch your tents, be sure that you are near some mountain or water, have sufficient victuals, and provide for more than you think that you will need. You shall have many machines of war running to make horrible sounds to frighten your enemies. In battle you should have all manners of arms. Some of the army will stay in one place and others shall go all about. You will have towers of movable trees over all with well armed knights therein, archers, crossbow men, and lancers with burning darts. If you see them fearful or doubtful, comfort their hearts by good and cheerful teaching. You will order your knights in this manner: on the right hand of your enemies, the swordsmen, on the left hand, jousters with spears, and in the middle of those, the archers and criers with horrible voices that will cast brands of burning fire. At all times, if possible, you should be in a higher place than your enemies and if you see any battalion fail, help it instantly. Whatever part of your enemies that you see failing, hastens you to that part. Stability and tenacity are worth much to have victory over all things. Of this, men commonly say-and true it is-that one man may not overcome his enemies, unless he first overcomes cowardice. You should have many spies and ambushes with horrible sounds, for that is the most principal craftiness in battle to obtain victory. You shall have certain places ordained for the host for drinks and other necessities. You will have elephants to bear towers of trees and knights armed within them, for they are very horrible and bare great terror. Dromedaries and other swift beasts will be in the host to help those that need it. If you fight in a castle, you shall have poison darts and arrows and if you come to water, from which your enemies drink, poison it. Be not too hasty in your works and fight with every people in their manner. In all your works take counsel of astronomers, for all earthly things are governed by the stars and the stars make many actions in the hearts of men, for from that comes dissention, battles, victories, and discomforts.

Chapter 55: Physiognomy is a science necessary to know the manners of men

Often before we have said that diverse manners of people-counselors, knights, constables, marshals, notaries, messengers and others that will serve kings and emperors-should have certain characteristics, which have been aforesaid. However, as hard as it is to find and know characteristics, good virtues and the manners of people without lengthy proof, it is a very appropriate and profitable thing to every prince that he know the science of physiognomy by which he may know by sight, which manners and dispositions every man will have naturally. Therefore as we have said, it is to be known that all bodily things are governed and ordained by the planets and stars. Therefore every man, at the beginning of his birth, by the virtue of the stars, which had regard to him, then, is disposed to diverse virtues and vices. It is true as Bugusarus the philosopher says, in the beginning of the *Centiloquium of Ptolemy*, that every wise man has virtue and will by which he may keep himself in regards to his nature and the virtues of stars.[67] By example, this book tells us that at some time two philosophers/astronomers were lodged in a weaver's house. On that night a son was born to the weaver. The astronomers beheld the constellations of his birth by their castle and found that he should be wise, courteous, good of counsel and well-beloved of kings, and that thing they hid from the father. The child grew and his father and mother believed that they might well teach him their craft, but he wouldn't learn it for anything, not for beatings, threats, or fairness, and therefore they let him alone. Afterwards, this youth sent himself to school, became a good scholar, and learned the courses of the stars, law, and the governance of realms; he afterwards became a great lord in the realm. Another time the contrary befell the King of India's son. The king wanted his son to know philosophy and all sciences, and therefore he sent throughout India and in other countries for masters to teach his son learning, as applied to so great a king. But that did not help, for he would not turn his heart to the sciences of learning, but to handcrafts. Because of that, the king was sorrowful and troubled and he called to him all the wise men of his realm, and asked them how that this might be. All accorded that nature led the child to do that and often such cases have befallen.

Chapter 56: Examples to prove the aforesaid thing

The disciples of Hippocrates the wise painted an image in parchment, resembling Hippocrates and took it to Polemon who was a master of physiognomy.[68] He said, "Regard this figure and tell us the qualities, the manners, and the temperament of such a man as this figure presents."[69] He beheld quickly the figure and the making of all the body, and said, "Such a man is lecherous and deceitful." When the disciples heard that they would have killed him and they said to him, "O you fool, that is the figure and the image of the best man in the world." Polemon appeased them and said, "Whose image is this that you have showed me?" They said, "This is the semblance of the wise Hippocrates." He said, "Why would you ask me? I have answered you as I felt by my science." They returned again to their master Hippocrates and told him which Polemon said of his domain. Hippocrates said, "Truly it is all that Polemon says; nevertheless, since I understood all that, I took heed of things which I was inclined to and they were foul and reprehensible. I established my understanding as a king over all my body; I have withdrawn from all follies and I have had victory and mastery against all foolish delights." This is the commendation of Hippocrates the philosopher. Philosophy is no more than the love of knowledge and wisdom, the abstinence from folly, and victory over foolish will.

Chapter 57: Here is proved that the soul accords with the conditions of the body

It is a certain thing that the soul, which is the form of the body, follows the nature, temperament, and properties of the body. For often we obviously see that the hearts of men change themselves according to the passions of the body, and that appears in drunkenness, in love, in frenzy, in fear, in sorrowfulness, in desires, and in delights. For in all these passions of the body, the soul and the heart change them. Nature is so great a fellow between body and soul that the passions of the body change the soul and the passions of the soul change the body. That appears in the passion of drunkenness, which is of the body. Drunkenness makes for forgetting in the soul, by reason that the great smokes go up to the brain, and trouble the imagination, which serves the understanding, and present to it the likeness of bodily things. Thus it puts away all the remembrance of things that were understood beforehand and disturbs the knowledge of things that are to be understood. Moreover the soul is the beginning and the cause of all the natural movements of the body, yet, nevertheless, this virtue is taken away from him by drunkenness, which is a passion of the body. A drunken man, when he should go to his right hand, goes to his left hand. In the same manner we may show the contrary; it is to be known that the passions of the soul make the body change and his movements to vary. A man may see that openly in anger, in fear, and in love. These passions make great changes to the body, as every man knows that has experienced them; and this also appears in movements. If a man goes up a narrow tree and lies in a high place, often he falls only by his imagination and the thought of falling. If the same tree were on the ground, where here is no fear or danger, he would never fall. Moreover, we see that every beast has his proper soul and his proper body. These species never fail and it was never found that any beast had a body of one species and a soul of another species. It may not be that one beast has the body of a hart and a soul of a lion. Moreover, we see that knights know the goodness of horses and hunters know the goodness of hounds by their shapes and abilities. Of all these aforesaid things, we may reasonably conclude that the fellowship and the accord between the soul and the body is so great and so much confirmed and established by nature, that in the passions of one the other is a partaker or a sharer[70]. Every body has a proper soul and every beast has a proper manner and condition, in diverse species, as among horses, one is less than the other in movement or in color and as we have previously said in the same manner of beasts, we have showed this without doubt in many species. One man has one manner and condition and another has another manner and condition, in figure and in face; and by the other things that appear in the body, a man may judge the conditions and manners that he has or should have by nature. Aristotle proves this at the beginning of his physiognomy, translated out of Greek into Latin.

Chapter 58: The science of physiognomy

Physiognomy is a science to judge the conditions or virtues and manners of people, after the tokens or signs that appear in the fashion or making of the body, and namely of the face, the voice, and the color. One easy and general manner of physiognomy is to judge the virtues and the manners of man after the temperament. There are four temperaments, for a man is sanguine, phlegmatic, choleric, or melancholy. These four temperaments of four humors of the body rise up and answer to the four elements and to the four times of the year. The blood is hot and moist in likeness to the air. Phlegm is cold and moist according to the nature of water. Choler is hot and dry after the nature of fire. Melancholy is cold and dry according to the nature of the earth. The sanguine, by nature, should love joy, laughing, the company of women, and much sleep and singing. He will be brave enough, of good will, and without malice. He will be fleshy and his temperament will be easy to hurt and to be impaired because of his tenderness. He will have a good stomach, good digestion, and good nimbleness, and if he is wounded, he will soon be whole. He will be generous, liberal, of fair appearance, and active enough of body. The phlegmatic by nature should be slow, sad, very quiet, slow to answer, feeble of body, and easy to fall with palsy. He will be large and fat and he will have a feeble stomach, feeble digestion, and good nimbleness. As pertaining to manners, he will be compassionate, chaste, and little desire the company of women. The choleric by nature should be lean of body. His body is hot and dry and he will be somewhat rough, easy to anger and easy to appease, of sharp wit, wise, of good memory, a great busybody, extravagant, foolhardy, nimble of body, and hasty of word and answer. He loves hasty vengeance and is desirous of the company of women more than he needs to be. He should have a good enough stomach, especially in cold times. The melancholy man should be lean of body and dry. He should have a good appetite for meat and commonly he is a glutton and has good activity of his belly. Pertaining to manners, he should be pensive and slow, of quiet will, quiet and fearful, and will meddle little. He is slower to anger than a choleric man, but he holds anger longer. He is of a subtle imagination as in handcrafts, and the melancholy men are well prone to be subtle workmen. The sanguine men should be ruddy of color, the phlegmatic should be white and pale, the choleric should have yellow color somewhat mixed with red, and the melancholic should be somewhat black and pale.

White color

White color somewhat mingled with red in a man is a sign that he is hot in nature, and of sanguine temperament; but red color is a sign that the temperament is well tempered, if such color is not rough in all the body. Aristotle speaks of this here shortly, but hereafter he will say it more openly.

Physiognomy of the hair

Soft hair is a sign of fearfulness and coarse hair is a sign of hardiness and strength and that appears in diverse beasts, for a hare and a sheep are very timid and have very soft hair.[71] And the lion and boar are very tough and have tough hair. Also in fowls, those that have coarse feathers by nature are strong and courageous as a cock, and those that have soft pins are fearful, as turtle doves are and quail[72]. So it is of diverse people according to the place that they dwell in. For those that dwell toward the north are strong and courageous and have hard hair, and those that dwell toward the south are timid and have soft hair as those of Ethiopia. Plenty of hair about the stomach is a sign of a talkative person who is full of words, and they are likened to birds that have plenty of feathers on the belly.

The temperament of skin, as follows

Hard flesh throughout all the body is a sign of a man with little understanding. Such are the great masses of the common people, which are of coarse understanding, but they are good to work. Skin in medium softness that is not slack is a sign of good understanding, but if it is very soft and slack as a woman's is, it is a sign of a changeable and variant man. But if such skin be found in a man of strong body that has strong extremities, that which I said before is not a sign.

Temperaments according to the Movements

Slow movements are a sign of a dull and slow understanding, and quick and nimble movements are signs of good understanding and a hasty wit.

The temperaments of voice as it follows here

A great and well-hardened voice, like a trumpet, is a sign of a brave and bold man. A small and feeble voice like a woman's is a sign of a cowardly man. Therefore, the strong and brave beasts have strong and high voices, such as lions, bulls, and hounds. Cocks, which are stronger and more courageous than others, sing higher and more strongly. We see the contrary in the hare.

The color of the face it is here to be known

When a man has a face like the color of the flame of fire, he is wrathful and by nature he should be easy to anger. The aforesaid signs of figures, movements, and likeness of face are most certain among all other signs. It is to be known that to judge a man after one sign.

The signs of a strong heart[73]

There are eleven signs of strength and courage. The first is coarse hair. The second is an even stature of body. The third is large stature of bones, ribs, hands and feet. The fourth is a large, retracted belly. The fifth is large, massive muscles. The sixth is a large, sinewy neck with not much fat. The seventh is a large and broad breast, elevated and somewhat fat. The eighth is large haunches of good proportion. The ninth is gray or brown eyes, like a camel's hair, that are not opened or closed too much. The tenth is brown color in all the body. The eleventh is a sharp, straight forehead, neither greatly lean, full, nor all wrinkled

The ten signs of a coward or a weakling, as follows[74]

The first sign is soft hair. The second is a drooping man that is not upright. The third is when the entrails of the stomach go up above the navel. The third is yellow color in the face mingled with paleness. The fifth is feeble and closed-looking eyes. The sixth is little extremities. The seventh is long and small hands. The eighth is small, feeble kidneys. The ninth is a man easily terrified. The tenth is an overly easy movement in color and appearance and that he has an appearance of being pensive and full of thoughts.

The signs of a good temperament

The first sign of a good temperament is moderate skin between soft and hard and especially between lean and fat. The second sign is that a man is lean in the neck and in the muscles of the body. The third is that the face is open and well-divided. The fourth is that the ribs are well divided or distinguished and well-shaped. The fifth is that a man has lively color. The sixth is that he has soft and tender skin. The seventh is that the back is not fleshy. The eighth is that the hair is not overly coarse, overly thin, or overly black. The ninth is that he has black or brown eyes that are somewhat moist.

The signs of an ill temperament

The first sign is a man overloaded with skin about the neck and the legs from the knees evilly separated. The second is a large, round, fleshy forehead like the drawn curve of a compass. The third is yellow eyes. The fourth is large and fleshy cheeks. The fifth is fleshy kidneys. The sixth is long legs. The seventh is a fat neck and the face is fleshy and straight.

The signs to know shameless men

First, he has open and glistening eyes; the eyelids are large, short, and full of blood, and the shoulders are high and upraised, with the body somewhat stooping.

The signs of honest men

The honest and shamefast man is circumspect and wise in all of his deeds and ruddy of color as the sanguine are. The face is round, the breast somewhat upraised, his speech is hesitating, and the voice is full and strong. The eyes are steadfast and somewhat brown, not glistening, not overly open or closed, and his eyes do not close too often. Those things are the signs of the eyes of a man that is fearful or vicious.

The signs of the courageous

The signs of the courageous are a large, fleshy, and full forehead and he looks not overly sharp as do mad men, nor overly deathly as does the coward. He is fair of face, well disposed, late of motion, and is slow to take action unless it is important.

The signs of the coward

These are the signs of the cowardly: a little, lean, and wrinkled face, little, dead looking eyes, and low and small of stature, and that of feeble motions.

The signs of the servile person

The signs of the servile person are unseemly and wrinkled eyes, the head bowing toward the right side, kneeling to every man for nothing, the actions of his hands and his movements are unseemly and ill regulated.

The bitter man

The signs of the bitter man are that he has the bowing head and the stooping of a pensive man that is full of thought. He is black of color and has a lean and wrinkled face that is not rough with smooth, black hair.

The angry man

The angry man is prone to be straight of body and courageous. It is to be known that he is full of hot spirit and therefore he is foolhardy, somewhat ruddy of color, with great, large shoulders, great, strong extremities, and the breast is not very rough; he has a seemly chin, according to the face, and flat hair. Whosoever does not anger himself when and where he should and against those with whom he should be angry, he is not a man of right wit. Thus I find it written, but I think that such anger should come from charity to suppress wrongs.

The kind man

The characteristics of the kind man are principally shown by his looks and that commonly he is fleshy and has moist skin. He is of average stature and well-measured. He has somewhat flat hair that is somewhat scarce.

The small heart

The signs of the small heart are a small face, small eyes, that all of the limbs of his body are small, and his skin is lean.

The contentious

The contentious are inclined to have large upper lips that protrude over the lower lips, with somewhat red faces. [Page 225]

The signs of the compassionate and merciful man

The compassionate and merciful man's signs are a white and clean color, the eyes are ready to weep, and they love gladly new and piteous stories that they remember. When they hear piteous stories they weep easily, especially after wine. They are perceptive without malice, they love women, and often they beget daughters. In *Proverbs* it is said that the compassionate man has three virtues that are to be known: wisdom, fear, and honesty. The tyrant or the cruel man has the contrary.

The lecher

The lecher is often white in color; the hair is rough, long, and black. He has rough temples and fat eyes that roll swiftly in sight like a madman. Beasts in rutting season have such a look.

The sleeper

The sleeper often times has a large head, a large neck, and somewhat fat in body and fleshy, and rough all about the belly.

The mindful man

Commonly they are of good minds that have the larger, stouter, and fleshier limbs from the joints upward than from the joints downwards. They have round heads well proportioned to the body.

Conditions of women

The most manifest difference in beasts is that one is male and the other is female. According to these differences we understand that the manners and virtues of each are changed, for among all beasts that are nourished or daunted by the knowledge of man, the females are the most humble, easy to teach, and the least worthy. And not for that, they are the most feeble of body and least powerful to defend themselves; it is the same in wild beasts. But women are more fickle and diverse, namely, than men are from other males, for as they are feebler of body and of temperament, so in the same manner they are endowed with less reason. Therefore they become angry easily and ask hastily for vengeance. Very badly can they withstand temptation and namely temptation of fleshly delight.

The signs of the feet

Whosoever has well-shaped feet with large and sinewy toes should be strong and brave for he has the characteristic of the male. He that has little, straight feet with short toes that are not sinewy and more delicate to the view than strong feet, he is feeble, cowardly, and like a woman. He that has crooked toes is commonly shameless and is in his manner, like birds that take their praise without shame.

The signs of the ankles

Those men who have obviously sinewy ankles should be courageous and they have the characteristic of the male. Those who have fleshy ankles that are not obvious are soft of heart and like women.

Signs of the leg

Those men who have well made, sinewy, and strong legs should be courageous and have the characteristics of the male. Those men who have small, sinewy legs are lecherous. Those men who have overly little knees are strong of heart as women are and that appears by their fashion.

Signs of the thighs

Those men who have bony and sinewy thighs are strong after the properties of the male. Those men who have fleshy thighs that are not bony are soft after the properties of women.

Signs of the breast

Those men who have bony and sharp chest should be strong. Those men who have fleshy and fat chest are soft men. Those that have little and dry flesh on the chest are ill mannered and are likened to apes.

The belly

Those men who have bellies that are moderately fat and not large are strong, of good temperament, and have the properties of the male. They who have lean and hungry bellies are soft.

The chin

Those men who have great chins are strong and brave and have the properties of the male. Those that have small and weak chins are soft and like women.

The ribs

Those men who have good ribs are strong and brave after the properties of the male. Those who have feeble ribs have the properties of women. Those that have ribs swelling outwards like they are swollen are talkative, foolish in words, and are like frogs and toads.

The shoulders

Those men, who have high and upraised shoulders with sinews and muscles appearing, are strong and brave after the properties of the male. Those that have the contrary have the properties of women. Those that have the shoulders hanging downward and well shaped are generous and liberal. Those who have the contrary are coarse and hungry.

The neck

Those men who have necks that are well preserved and are well distinguished by their joints are of good knowledge and understanding, for those are signs of good understanding and nimbleness of wit and signs that they perceive easily the motions of knowledge. Those that have necks of a contrary making and disposition have a slow wit. A great neck that is not fat is a sign of strength and hardiness after the properties of a man, and a small neck is the contrary. A great fleshy, short neck is a sign of anger like that of a bull. A long neck that is not overly large is a sign of courage like that of a lion. An overly short neck is a sign of a beguiler and a deceiver like a wolf.

The lips

Whosoever has lips on an average between thick and thin, and the upper lip comes down and closes on the lower lip, is courageous and brave, likened to the lion that a man may see in large and strong hounds.[75] Those that have thin lips that are hard about the teeth with the teeth upraised and outward is churlish and foul and likened to a pig. Those that have large lips with one hanging and descending over the other are fools and likened to asses. Those that have the upper lip turned upwards with the gums greatly elevated are disdainful and evil-sayers, likened to baying hounds

The nose

Those that have large noses are easily inclined towards greed, are disposed to concupiscence, and are likened to oxen. Those that have a tip of the nose that is large and round are rude of wit and likened to swine. Those that have a tip of the nose that is sharp are strongly angry and likened to hounds. Those that have round noses that are not sharp are brave and bold and are likened to lions. A drooping nose and broadness between the brows are signs of a courageous man and he is likened to the eagle. Those that have a nose that is crooked and a forehead that is round and pointed upward are lecherous, angry, and likened to apes. Open nostrils are signs of the angry, for when a man is angry, his nostrils flare.

The face

Those that have great and fleshy faces are disposed to concupiscence or lusts of the flesh. A lean face is a sign of study and concern. A fat face is a sign of fearfulness. A little face is a sign of a little heart. A great and broad face is a sign of sloth in the manner of oxen and asses. A straight, little face of poor appearance is a sign of a hard and hungry heart. An open and fair appearance is a sign of a generous heart. A little, small forehead is a sign of little wit, ill characteristics, and they are hard to teach. An all round forehead is a sign of a coarse wit. A longer than normal forehead is a sign of a slow wit. A square forehead of average size is a sign of fairness and courage. A plain and straight forehead is a sign of a flatterer. The forehead that is somewhat troubled in appearance is a sign of fieriness and hardiness.

The eyes

Those that have red eyelids love wine commonly well and are great drinkers. Heavy eyelids are signs of a good sleeper. Little eyes are signs of a little and slow heart. Large eyes are signs of a violent wit. Average eyes, neither large nor small, are signs of a good temperament that is without vice. Deep eyes are signs of malice; overly opened eyes, like they are thrust outward, commonly are signs of a fool. Somewhat deep eyes are signs of hardiness, but eyes that are average, that is, neither too deep nor too far out, are best.

The ears

Little ears are signs of good understanding. Large ears are signs of dull understanding. Average ears are best.

The color

Those men that are overly black are fearful and likened to the Egyptians and Ethiopians, and those that are overly white are fearful like women. Those that are of average color between black and white are strong and brave. Those that are yellow of color are courageous like the lions. Those that are red men are perceptive and treacherous, full of craftiness like foxes. Those that are pale and troubled in color are fearful for they bear the color of fear in their foreheads. Those that are red in color are hasty and eager, for when a man is chafed by running or other motions he turns red. Those that have a flame color like the light of a fire become mad easily. Those that have such color about the chest are always angry and that appears so, for when a man is very angry he feels the breast all aflame. Those men that have large ruddy veins about the neck and the temples are passionate and very angry, and that appears so, for a man that is angry has the same passion. Those that have a somewhat ruddy face are modest and it is a sign of honesty showing in their face. Those that have the cheeks all red as if they were drunk show signs that they love good wine very well.

The color of the eyes

Those that have very black eyes show signs that they are cowardly for black color approaches nigh to darkness and in darkness a man is more easily afraid than in light. Those that have eyes not very black that decline to yellow are of a good heart. Speckled eyes and white eyes are signs of fearfulness, for white color is a sign of fear. Those that have eyes of the color of camel hair are courageous and likened to the lion and the eagle. Those that have eyes colored like red wine are disposed to madness and likened to beasts that may not be daunted. Those that have eyes like the lights of a sparkling, flaming fire are angry, shameless, and likened to hounds. Those that have troubled and discolored eyes show signs of fear, for he that is afraid turns pale, and those that have shining eyes are lechers likened to rooks and cocks.

The signification of various limbs

Those that have rough legs are lecherous, and those that have the breast and the belly very rough are very unstable and variant. Those that have the neck that is rough on the back are liberal and likened to lions. Those that have sharp chins are of good courage and likened to hounds. Those that have the brows near together are heavy and sorrowful, for they bear the signs thereof. Whosoever has their brows sticking up against the nose and into the temples on each side are foolish and likened to swine. Those that have their hair standing up are fearful, and that appears so, for those who are afraid have their hair sticking up. Those that have their locks or hair curly show signs of fearfulness, but locks that are curly towards their ends show signs of good courage. Those that have their foreheads upraised beforehand are generous and likened to lions. Those that have a longhead and their ears growing towards their forehead near to the nose are slow of wit. The round head, as we have said before, is more of a sign of knowledge.

Signs of movements

Those that hold the muscles of their shoulders right straight when they move themselves show signs that they are strong and brave and they are likened to horses. Those that have little feet and feeble legs are feeble and faint like women. Those that have eyes that move much are sharp and ravenous like the goshawk. Those that often close their eyes are fearful. Those that in looking or in regarding fix their sight and hold it steady are studious and of good understanding and that appears so, for when a man studies deeply, he holds his sight steady.

The voice

Those that have a great and horrible voice, not very high, do wrongs gladly and are likened to asses. Those whose voice at the beginning of a word is great and low and ends all small and high have the nature of oxen and are angry. Those that have a high voice, small, sweet, and pleasant are soft, have little manhood, and are likened to women. A great high and strong voice is a sign of a strong, brave man that is likened to a lion and to a strong hound. A softly breaking, pleasant voice is a sign of a gentle and well-mannered man. A small, high, strong voice is a sign of a man easy to anger.

Signs of the body

Those that have a little body are sharp in body and wit because their hearts are near the extremities. Therefore, in a short time, they move themselves and the virtue of the heart spreads throughout all the body, and it goes to the brain where the understanding is fulfilled. Those that are very large of body are slow, and their bodies and understanding tarry because their hearts are far from the extremities of their bodies and the brain. Those that have hot, dry flesh and are little of body are variant and unstable and hence, they may not fulfill that thing which they have begun because they put themselves to other things. Those that are large and have moist skin with little heat are slow and have slow understanding. Those that are large of body and have dry skin and color according to the heat are of high understanding and very capable of fulfilling what they think; for though they are large, they have the body and the temperament well proportioned. But among all others, those of best temperament are not overly large or overly small. Those who are ill measured of body are disposed to treachery and other ill teachings. Those who are well measured of body are just and rightful men. By that which we have said before, it appears that all physiognomy takes heed of four things. First are the properties of male and female; the second is the aforesaid disposition of the body of man; the third is the fashion and form of man and his likeness to the manner of other beasts; and the fourth is the sign of the appearance or likeness of the passion by which a man is known. Though there are many tokens or signs by which a man may judge the physiognomy, nevertheless, some are more certain and apparent than others. The signs that are in the head are the most principal; the signs that are about the eyes, the head and the face, hold the first and chief degree of judgment. The signs that are about the chest and shoulders hold the second degree. The third degree holds the signs that are about the legs and the feet. The signs that are about the belly hold the fourth degree and are the least certain. As the manners of signs accord, the more certain the judgment is.

Chapter 59: Now gracious lord, I will translate the science of physiognomy to you in a shorter manner, for some books of Aristotle's making have that science shorter than others, and so you may choose which best pleases you

It is to be known that the seed within the womb is digested, like a mass within a boiling pot, and therefore pale color and sadness are signs that the concoction is not perfect. Therefore, if you find such color in a man, he is a little man, these are signs that the perfection of his nature is made less and diminished. Such a man you will shun for he is disposed to ill teachings. When you see a man that often regards you and when you regard him he fears and grows ruddy, and especially if he sighs, and in his face he takes to weeping at the eyes, that man loves and fears you. If he has characteristics that are the contrary, he thinks little of you and is envious. And just as he that has a fault of nature of a lively color is to be shunned, even more, is he to be shunned, who lacks any limb at birth or whose limbs are unnaturally deformed in any other manner, such men are to be shunned as enemies, for they are inclined to wickedness.

He that has a moderate temperament, is of average stature, has gray eyes, brown locks, a laughing face, brown color or yellow blended with red, a body all whole and well proportioned, the right stature, a head of average size, a voice not overly great or overly small but average and very hard and is sparing of speech unless it is needed, you should have him in your company.

Hair

Plenty of soft locks are a sign of gentleness and a cold brain. Plenty of hair on both shoulders is a sign of folly and ignorance. Plenty of hair on the belly and chest are signs of horribleness and a singularity of nature, little understanding, and a love of the body. Red color is the sign of a man that is angry and vicious. Brown and auburn locks are signs of a love of right and justice.

Eyes

Whosoever has very large eyes, especially if they are pale, is envious, immodest, slow and disobedient. He that has eyes of average size, which are black or gray, has courtesy, perceptive understanding, and is true. Whosoever has long, straight eyes and whose face is very straight is malicious and felonious. Whosoever has eyes like an ass is a sot and and has coarse understanding. Whosoever has moving, flying eyes that are sharp looking is a deceiver, a thief, and a beguiler. He that has red sparkling eyes is fierce and courageous. He that has eyes that are white with freckles or spots, or that has black or red scattered through the eyes, is most to blame among all others and is the most reprovable; such a man is the worst among all others.

Brows

Whosoever has very rough brows lacks eloquence. He that has large brows stretching to the temples is foul and lecherous. He that has brows not overly thick with hair, of average length, and that are large enough is of good understanding and easily comprehends.

Nose

He that has a small, sharp nose is angry. He that has a long nose that is somewhat stooping and stretches towards the mouth is worthy and brave. He that has a crooked nose is hasty, malicious, and angry. Whosoever has his nostrils very open is strongly angry. Whosoever has a low, flat nose in the middle that stoops toward the tip is a trickster and a liar. The nose that is most praiseworthy is of average length and breath, the tip is not overly sloping, overly flat or stooping, and the nostrils are of average size.

Face

Whosoever has a plain face that is not fleshy is an argumentative, quarrelsome fellow, ill taught, wrongful, and foul. Whosoever has a face that is average in cheeks and temples and that is somewhat fat is truthful, praiseworthy, understanding, wise, companionable, honest, and of good intelligence. Whosoever has a large mouth is chivalrous and brave. Whosoever has large, swollen lips is a fool. Whosoever has an overly fleshy and large face is unwise, envious, and a liar. Whosoever has a straight, well-proportioned face is wise, ready in his deeds, and of subtle understanding. Whosoever has a small, straight face that is yellow and discolored is very malicious, full of vices, a deceiver, and a drunkard. Whosoever has a long and straight face is angry. Whosoever has swollen temples and cheeks is very angry. Whosoever has very large ears is a fool except in that which he has learned, and of that, which he has learned and understood, he holds it well and remembers it well. Whosoever has small ears is a sot, a thief, and a lecher.

Voice

Whosoever has a great, pleasant voice that is well hardened is chivalrous, pleasant, and eloquent. Whosoever has an average voice that is between great and small is wise, prudent, veritable, and rightful. Whosoever has the hasty word, if he has a small voice, he is angry, foolish, envious, and a liar, and if his voice is great, he is angry and hasty. Whosoever has a very sweet voice is envious and suspicious. A very great sweetness of voice is a sign of folly and ignorance. Whosoever moves his hands often while speaking and makes many gestures is envious. A soft speaker is a deceiver and he that speaks without moving the hands and without gestures and countenances is of perfect understanding, well disposed and of whole counsel.

Neck

Whosoever has a small neck should have a sweet voice that is well hardened, but he is unwise. Whosoever has a very short neck is treacherous, a braggart, and a deceiver. Whosoever has a very great neck is a fool and a glutton. Whosoever has a large belly is proud, a sot without discretion, and a lecher, but an average belly and chest are signs of highness of understanding and counsel. A broad chest highly upraised with a great closeness of the shoulders and the chin is a sign of prowess, hardiness, retention of understanding and knowledge. When back and the chin are overly small, they are signs of feebleness and a discordant nature. An average chest and chin are good signs and are to be praised.

The shoulders

When the shoulders are much upraised, it is a sign of a horrible nature and a liar. When the arms are long and reach to the knees when straight, it is a sign of hardiness, prowess, and generosity. When the arms are very short it is a sign of a love of discord and of ignorance. Long palms and a long back are signs of a good disposition towards many crafts, especially of handicrafts, and a sign of good governance. A short, large back is a sign of folly and of ignorance.

The feet

Large, fleshy feet are a sign of folly and a love for wrongs. Feeble, little feet are signs of feebleness in one's nature. Very small legs are signs of ignorance; large legs are signs of strength and hardiness. Great broadness in the heels and legs are signs of feebleness in natural virtue, and those that have them are soft in the manner of women. Whosoever has a wide, slow step is wise and very fast in all of his deeds, and whosoever has a small, swift step is suspicious, of evil will, and is empowered to inflict pain.

He is well disposed after his nature that has tender skin, a body neither overly rough or plain, average stature, lively color that is somewhat mingled with red, kind-looking, plenty of plain locks without many curls, eyes somewhat red that are open and large enough, a round head of average size, an evenly well-disposed neck, a well-proportioned head, shoulders somewhat hanging, legs and knees that are sinewy and not fleshy, a voice that is clear and tempered between great and small, long and broad palms, a back that is neither overly large or small, of little laughing, of fair appearance, and somewhat joyous. I have told you many signs, but you will not give a judgment or a sentence soon because of one of the signs. You will gather the witnesses of all the signs and if they are contrary, then you will judge from the majority of the signs and by those that are the truest as they accord.

Chapter 60: Here ends the treatise of physiognomy and begins the treatise of the governance of health for man's body according to natural science

Health is most desired among all things, for a man who is sorely sick has nothing that he would not give to have health and maintain it. What would it be worth to have the entire world, but to languish in sickness? Certainly little or nothing, for sickness enfeebles not only the body but also wise reason and the mind. Therefore every man, but especially princes and great lords, needs to have health and bodily strength for the common profit of the people. And that he knows how to keep himself in health of body so that he will not ever be in the keeping of physicians like a child is a ward of his tutor. Therefore gracious lord, I, James, your aforesaid servant, have translated for your excellence, in the previous book, the teachings of diverse authorities and examples on how you will keep your soul from vices and ill manners and how to live virtuously.

Chapter 61: Now I translate to you, from Latin into English, the teachings which will keep your health of body and heart so that you may, more worthily by bounty and nimbleness, govern all that is in your jurisdiction

All the wise philosophers, in one accord, say that there are four elements in the world from which every corruptible thing is made and namely are to be known: earth, water, air, and fire. Every one of these has two properties. The earth is cold and dry. Water is cold and moist. Air is hot and moist. Fire is hot and dry. In the body of every man are four humors answering to the four elements, and they have the same properties. Melancholy is cold and dry. Phlegm is cold and moist. Sanguine is hot and moist. Choleric is hot and dry. Because these properties are contrary, the body may not endure always, but it must return to the four elements from which it was made. Even though the body may not always last, it may last a long time if the nature of man is well nourished in due manner, by eating and drinking, just as we see the lighted wick of a candle that is nourished by the oil that is around it. If the oil was not there the wick would soon be burned and destroyed. In the same manner, if meat and drink did not nourish the natural heat, in a short time it would destroy the body. Beyond that, it must have moderation and proportion for if the wick is set overly deep in the oil it will soon be extinguished. If a man has an excess of meat and drink, the natural heat will be enfeebled, and because of that, soon after a man may fall into sickness and die. For Solomon says, "Many people perish from gluttony." Moderation in all things maintains health. Therefore, have moderation in meat and drink, in sleeping, in waking, in travail, in rest, in blood-letting, and in all other things. Whosoever does not do this will suddenly fall to various sicknesses. Whosoever may not stay within the right proportions, let him hold rather to too little than to too much. The deficiency may be restored more easily that the superfluity can be put away. It is written of Hippocrates, the wise physician, that he practiced great abstinence and therefore in a certain time he grew feeble of body. One of his disciples said to him, "Fair master, if you would eat well, you would not be so feeble." Hippocrates answered, "Fair son, I would eat to live, and not live to eat." It is well known that those men, which keep a reasonable diet and live moderately, are more whole of body, of better understanding, more nimble, stronger, livelier, more patient during travails and discomforts, and are of much longer life.

Chapter 62: Two principal things that maintain health

Two things are principally necessary to maintain the health of the body. The first is that a man uses meat and drink appropriately and according to his nature or kind and to his temperament, as in time, in hour, in season and according to his custom. Hippocrates says, "Custom is the second nature or kind." The second thing is that a man purge himself, in due time, of corrupt and superfluous humors, and therefore he should know that according to the four humors, the temperament diverges and varies; for some men are sanguine and others are phlegmatic. The third are choleric and the fourth are melancholic. In this manner, nature diversifies meats according to hot, cold, moist and dry. A man is whole of body that does not stray from evenness and right measure and while temperament holds him in good condition. Therefore a man should use meats according to his temperament, but when the temperament surpasses moderation, there it is appropriate to use meats, to remove or bring the temperament to evenness and moderation. It must be done easily, little by little, so that one's nature is not grieved, for one's nature hates sudden change. I will you tell an example so that you may understand it better. The choleric is hot and dry and the phlegmatic is moist and cold; therefore each one may use meats of one manner of nature appropriate to each, while no humor sins in them by excess. But when the humors pass the right measures by disrupted diet or nature of time or of region, they should use contrary diets to redress the excess and the surfeit. The choleric should use a cold and moist diet, and the phlegmatic should use a dry and hot diet. In a like manner diversity of diet should match the diversity of age, time, region and customs. One manner of diet is appropriate to young men, and another is appropriate to old men. Young men should have a large and moist diet; old men should have a subtle and hot diet. In spring, diet in moderation. In autumn, the diet should consist of hot and moist meats. In winter, a hot diet should be large and dry. In summer, the diet should be subtle, cold, and moist. In the region of the north, the diet should be great and hot. In the region of the south, the diet should be subtle and temperate. Those that are inclined much towards hard work should use a large and strong diet to digest it. Those that are inclined to rest much, a subtle and light diet is best to digest. Moreover, it is to be known that those men that have a hot and strong temperament and have large openings through all the body that scholars call pores, should use great meats and in large quantity. However, those men that have a body that is more lean with narrow openings should use a subtle diet in little quantity for large overtures are a sign that the natural heat is of great virtue, therefore, it calls for a great diet of great sustenance. Narrow overtures are a sign of the contrary and therefore he needs a contrary diet. Such diversity a man may find in diverse stomachs; for those that have a hot and strong stomach, it is best to use a large and strong diet, for such a stomach is like a great fire that has the power to burn a great amount of wood and logs. However, when the stomach is cold and feeble, the diet should be subtle and light for such a stomach is likened to the small fire that may burn only flax or straw. It is to be known that at times it is found that all of the body of a man is hot and not because the stomach is cold. The signs of a good stomach are lightness of body, good appetite for meat, and clearness of understanding. The signs of a bad stomach are heaviness of body, sloth, a discolored face, heaviness of eye, flatulence, swelling of the belly, a lack of appetite, or a lust to eat often, and a sudden stretching of the arms and all of the body.

Chapter 63: The governance of the body of man regarding sleep to maintain health

When a man rises from sleep, he should walk a little, dally about, stretch his limbs evenly, for that strengthens the body and revives the head, so that the vapors that go up into the head in the time of sleeping may have issue. In summer it is good to wash the extremities with cold water to hold the natural heat within the body, and that will cause an appetite to eat. After that he should rub his gums with leaves of a tree which is of a hot and dry nature, for that cleans the teeth, amends the tongue, clears the speaking, gives a good appetite for meat, and makes good breath. After that a man should use the fumigation of herbs according to the time and to his temperament, for that opens the closures of the brain, it clarifies the face and the sight, and it causes a man to grow gray later. When this is done a man should anoint himself with good ointments according to the season. Such ointments should be of good odor, for that comforts the body a long time, and it makes the body light and free. The good odor comforts the spirits and makes the heart open and close, and because of the joy of the heart, the blood runs into the veins throughout all the body; for as physicians say, the blood is the friend of nature. After that, a man should use electuaries after the time and his temperament. The electuary is worth much if made with aloe, for aloe comforts the stomach and procures digestion.[76] It is good against feebleness of the heart and brain, against heartburn, and all the passions of the heart and brain. Whosoever does not have a place where he may make the electuary, then boil aloe in wine and drink it early. Rhubarb, the price of three or four pennies, should be taken early. It purges choler, withdraws the flame from the mouth of the stomach, increases the natural heat, drives away flatulence, and it makes the mouth savory. Also, fair things and honest clothing naturally delight man's heart.

Chapter 64: The rightful hours and times for eating and drinking

The rightful hour for eating is when the stomach is purged, cleansed, and void of meat, by appetite and desire that a man has to eat, and by subtle and thin spittle that descends or comes down from the palate of the mouth to the tongue. Whosoever eats before the digestion is finished does not help the natural course, but overtaxes it. Because of this, the natural heat will be of little good and so the meat will stay, long congealed in the stomach, and diverse sicknesses will arise from it. But whosoever eats at the aforesaid right hour feeds the natural heat, which is the instrument of nature to turn the meat and drink into flesh, blood, and bones. Therefore, to keep nature's heat and to void the stomach, it is good before eating meat to walk or ride somewhat, but it is better to walk than ride so that the natural heat is comforted by the motion. If anything is left in the stomach, it may descend to the bottom of the stomach, for the bottom of the stomach is hotter than the entrance and that which is in the bowel will also descend; then the belly may be purged more easily. Exercising before meat drives away flatulence, redresses the body, strengthens it, and makes all the body active. It comforts the natural heat and destroys ill humors. When a man has an appetite to eat, he should eat soon, for if he does not, the stomach will soon be replete or filled with humors. The stomach will then draw to itself the superfluities of the body, and afterwards, it will send fumes up to the brain and trouble and grieve it and make the head ache. When a man sits at a meal and diverse manners of meats are set before him, he should chose that which his heart guides him best to eat. The bread should be made of wheat and evenly leavened. He will begin with soft meat so that the issue of the stomach will be not obstructed. The wine should be good and tried, the flesh of the season well contrived. Afterwards, eat meat that is more binding and less of a laxative. At all times eat first that meat which is moist, easy to digest and after that, the greater meat. For if a man eats great meats first and then eats light meats, the light meat will soon be digested and it will not be able to descend to the bowels; therefore, they will turn, by corruption, into evil humors. However, if the light meat is first, when it is digested it will descend into the bowels and then the great meat will go the same way in its time without obstruction. It is to be known that the stomach is hotter at its bottom than about its mouth, for the bottom is fleshy and very near the liver and the gall and it receives heat from them. But the entrance of the stomach is sinewy and is more distant from the liver and the gall and the sinews are of a cold nature and the flesh is of a hot nature. When a man sits at a meal he should withdraw his hand before he is full and he should cease while he has his appetite. Whosoever does otherwise will soon be sick, his body will be grieved and his heart will hurt. Whosoever drinks water with meat or soon after will hurt for that quenches the natural heat, disturbs the digestion, and turns the meat into corruption. Whosoever needs to do that, drink a little that is temperately cold and if it is mixed with wine, it would be less to fear.

Chapter 65: Now it is to be known: the governance of the body regarding food

When a lord has eaten, it is good to stand awhile and to walk softly. Walk not upon hard earth or pavement, but upon earth softly covered with straw or rushes, for that will make the meat easy to descend little by little into the bottom of the stomach. Since it is good to rest and to sleep in a soft bed, in fresh clothes with a good odor, sleep first upon the right side and later upon the left side. End your sleep on your left side for that side is the most cold and most needs to be warmed. Sleeping before meat dries the moisture from the body and makes it lean, but sleeping after meat nourishes the body and gives it strength. All the senses rest while a man sleeps, and the natural heat returns that spreads abroad through all the body and to the five senses. This serves the stomach and the entrails for then they gather their strength and virtue, which was diminished and enfeebled when it was attending to all the senses and motions of the body. Therefore some philosophers say that it is more wholesome for the body to eat at evensong time than at midday, for at midday the five senses are working hard and that works the heart of man hard. Also by sleeping, by thought, and by diverse other things that a man has to do in times by the heat of the sun, which more shows his virtue at that time of the day. Therefore the natural heat at midday is less strong and the stomach has less power to digest the meat. But at evening we see all the contrary; for at that time, the five senses rest themselves from their hard labor, the discomforts of the day are passed, and night that is granted for rest comes. The cold of the night chases the natural heat toward the stomach and the entrails, and by so much it helps the digestive power that was disturbed by the heat of the sun which draws to itself the natural heat of the extremities of the body, for natural heat draws heat and cold disturbs it. It is to be known that to keep custom is worth much to maintain health, such that it is not excessive, and then it should not be changed suddenly from what is accustomed, but slowly, little by little. Therefore he that is accustomed to eat two times in the day, if he withdraws suddenly he may soon experience harm. That man who was inclined to eat but once and afterwards eats two times in one day may have much to fear, for the stomach will be troubled to receive more of a burden than it is used to receiving. Also, it is to be known that he that changes the hour of eating will feel harm from his nature by reason of both these things, for custom is the second nature and therefore whosoever changes custom hastily will experience harm as if the nature or temperament were changed. That which is said of meat and drink will be understood in the same manner of other customs, as in sleeping, hard work, resting, and all other things.

Chapter 66: The four parts of the year after their natures

All the old philosophers divide the year into four parts that are called spring, summer, autumn, and winter. These four times have properties that are likened to the four elements and to the four temperaments of which I have told before. The compositors say that spring begins at the feast that we call by the calendar, "Cathedra Sancti Petri," and it lasts until the feast of St. Urban. Then summer begins and it lasts until the feast of St. Symphoriane. Then autumn begins and it lasts until the feast of St. Clement. From there, winter lasts until the feast of the aforesaid St. Peter. The time of spring is hot and moist, as the air is, and therefore in that time all things begin to renew, to grow new, and to return to their normal conditions. The tempests begin to withdraw, the snows melt in the mountains, the rivers run into the hills, the wells spring up, the humors of trees and herbs ascend from the roots into the boughs, the seeds rise up, the grains grow, the meadows grow green, the flowers color the earth, the trees clothe themselves with leaves, buds, and sprouts, the beasts reproduce, and all living things take their virtues again. The birds sing, the nightingale shows his organ notes, all the earth receives its adornment and its beauty, and is like a fair young man that arrays himself well in all manner of adornment to show himself at a wedding. For as much as this time is hot and moist, the blood of man which is of similar temperament, grows in this season more than in any other time of the year and spreads through him to all the limbs of the body. In this time it is good to eat temperate meats, such as chicken, wild lettuce that is called escarole, and to drink milk from a goat and good wine in moderation. No time is more suitable to let blood, especially of the body, purgation of the belly, the company of women, sweat-baths, potions or drinks of spices. Medicines and laxatives should be used in this time. For all that is voided by bloodletting or by other medicines, this time hastily restores by its heat and its moisture.

Chapter 67: Summer[77]

Summer begins at the feast of St. Urban and lasts until the feast of St. Symphoriane. In this time the days grow long and the nights grow short. The heat is increased in all regions, the torments of the air are assuaged, the sea grows calm, the snakes grow, the vines grow, and the corn grows ripe. Then the world seems to be a spouse that is fully-grown in body and is the perfect age in full virtue of its natural heat. The time of summer is hot and dry and therefore red choler reigns then. Summer has the same condition and because of that a man should shun hot and dry meats, which engender red choler. A man should eat meats of a cold and moist temperament so that his nature does not rightfully pass what is moderate, such as: flesh of calves, vinegar, lobster, pôts of oatmeal, gourds, pomegranates, and similar other meat. Also drink in moderation, green wine that is clear, sharp, and sparkling. Also know that a man may use meats in moderation as long as they are not overly cold or overly hot, for man's natural heat is feebler in summer than in other times. A man needs to have more abstinence in that time than in winter, when by reason, the stomach is hotter than in cold time and the cold chases the natural heat from the other limbs that are within the body. A man should scarcely and seldom use the company of women, exercise, and sweat baths. Avoid great distress and do not practice letting of the blood unless there is a great need.

Chapter: 68: Autumn

Autumn begins at the feast of St. Symphoriane and lasts until the feast of St. Clement. Then the days grow shorter than they were and the nights grow longer. But as spring falls on the equinox, that is to say the evenness of day and night, so it is in autumn; but in spring, the days grow longer from the equinox forward and the nights grow shorter. In autumn, the contrary happens. In this time the air grows cold and dry, the north wind blows often, wells diminish, green things fade, fruits fall, the air loses its beauty, the birds seek hot regions, the beasts desire their lairs, and snakes go to their ditches. Then the world seems as a woman of great age that now grows cold and needs to be clothed warmly because youth has passed and age draws nigh. Therefore it is no marvel that she has lost her beauty. This time is dry and cold by nature and then reigns black choler, which is called melancholy. Therefore, at this time, one needs to use hot and moist meat, such as well cooked chicken, yearling lambs, partridges, doves, good, sweet, and ripe wine that well nourishes the body, figs, dates, and raisins. Shun all meat that generates melancholy; about which I shall tell you after this. A man may, without the peril, work harder and keep more company with women than in summer. A man may use baths and laxatives in this time if needed. If a man has a need to vomit, let it be done at midday when the sun is most hot, for at that hour the superfluities are gathered. Medicinal purgations and things that purge melancholy, such as agarik and others that are similar, should be made in this time.[78] Agarik purges phlegm and melancholy.

Chapter 69: Winter

Winter begins at the feast of St. Clement and lasts until the feast of St. Peter as was said before. In this time the days are wonderfully short and the nights long, for the sun lowers itself from our region. Therefore the cold is great, the winds are sharp, the storms of the air are hideous and horrible, the trees are despoiled of their leaves and all their green has faded, except from the pines, laurels, olives and a few other trees. Many beasts hide themselves in caves of mountains in order to flee and shun the cold and moistness. The air becomes dark and foul and beasts that have no lair, tremble, become impaired, and mourn from the cold and moistness, which is killing and contrary to life. Therefore, all that is dead soon grows cold. In this time the world seems like an old cat, all overcome with age and travail, that might not live for she is all despoiled of beauty, strength, and virtue. Winter is a cold and moist time; therefore it is good to use hot meats, such as flesh of mutton, fat capons, and roasted flesh, which is hotter than it is in a pot or boiled in water, figs, raisins, nuts, and good, strong, and clear red wine. Electuaries are good in this time and a good fire of coal and of dry wood that is in season. But a fire with smoke is not appropriate in any season or place, except in Hell only. A man may use exercise and the company of women without excess and more than in summer, autumn, or spring. In no time of the year should a man eat so much as in the winter, for the great cold air makes the natural heat withdraw and return to the stomach and the entrails, and therefore digestion is better and more virtuous in winter than in any other time. But in spring and in summer, the belly and the stomach are colder, for in the heat of that time natural heat spreads throughout all the body and by this, the stomach grows colder, the digestion is disturbed, and the humors turn into corruption. As it is to be known that as long as the natural heat endures in right moderation by a balance of the four humors, the health of man will be kept, for the nature of man fails in two manners. One manner is by great age and that is called natural death, for nature desires that every thing that is made of the four elements, which are contrary, may not endure for all time. That other manner is by ill keeping, where sickness and soreness come from and which leads to death. Such death is called a death of accident and out of nature, because nature might have endured longer if it had been well governed, as it should have been.

Chapter 70: Things that make the body fat, moist, and well disposed

The body of man and all that is made from the four elements are governed according to the motions of Heaven, and according to the same motions the time varies. Therefore in different times we should have different care. Nonetheless, some things have their effect, more or less every day of the year, as sleep nourishes the body every time of the year and much waking makes the body lean and destroys it. Therefore, gracious lord, as I find written, I shall tell you shortly what things make the body fat, moist, and well disposed and what things do the contrary. The body makes itself fat, moist, and well disposed with good meat and drink according to the many temperaments after the time of the year and the hour of the day accustomed or used, as aforesaid. Above all things, they are the rest of the body, gladness of heart, joyful fellowship or company, hot and moist meat, drinks of good and ripe wine, sweet milk and hot drink made with honey, tender bread made from the flour of wheat, moderate sleep after meat upon a soft bed and in a temperate place, cold baths in water that is moderately cold in temperature, sitting in a bath for a short time so that nature is not enfeebled, the use of ointments according to the time and temperament, and the smell of sweet odors according to the time. In winter, the odor of hot things is good, such as aloes and other things that are similar. In summer, it is the odor of cold things such as rose and violet. Have a vomit at least once in every month, for vomiting purges the stomach of ill humors above, as a medicine or a laxative does beneath. When the ill humors are put away, the natural heat will be comforted enough to digest the meat. To these things it helps much to have riches and glory, victory upon enemies, and to have hope and trust in the people that are under your governance. Delight in honest actions and behold it, as to see horses run, younglings skirmish, and beasts chased in the hunt. Above all things, behold often fair things, make fair works, devise delightful- songs to hear and sing, read and study good books, laugh and play with dear and well beloved people, find solace in diverse instruments of music, such as harps and other similar instruments, and wear different clothes that are good, fair and of diverse colors and cloths, changing them often. These are the things that comfort the heart, make the body fat, whole, and well disposed.

Chapter 71: Things that do the contrary

These are the things that do the contrary to the aforesaid things: small amounts of meat which are not nourishing, little to drink that is especially feeble, much travail, great journeys made, to be in the sun a long time in hot weather, sleep before meat, walking upon hard pavement, bathing in salt water or in water in which there is brimstone, much use of salted meat, to drink much overly old wine, too many purgatives through the belly, and much bleeding at diverse times. Above all things that enfeeble the body and destroy the spirits: much waking, too much thought, using the company of women too much, great dread, much doubting, being angry often, and holding anger a long time, greatly desiring goods of fortune, thinking of hatred and vengeance often, making great sorrow over the loss of goods, foul and unseemly things to behold, hearing songs of dolor, hearing evil things, and remembering misfortunes.

From all manner of mischief, almighty God defend our liege lord, King Henry the Fifth, and James le Butler, Earl of Ormond, his lieutenant of Ireland, who commanded me to translate this book. And grant them, great God, and all their subjects, to grow in the seven virtues and grace at all times. Amen. **Laus deo clementissimo.**

Thanks be to God that is so kind

That of this work He has made an end.

Notes

---

[1] Cicero is originally Tully in the text, but Yonge uses Cicero as a paraphrase in the margins, therefore Cicero will be used throughout the remainder of this document.

[2] The original phrase was "parcewynge engyn." The use of the translated word, perceiving, in this instance, requires this particular definition of engine.

[3] According to Stephen Williams in his *The Secret of Secrets*, Aristotle was allegedly "too old and infirm" to accompany Alexander on his campaigns in Asia (8).

[4] The original word used for "munificence" is "folargesse" which has no one word equivalent in Modern English, hence the use of a more descriptive phrase.

[5] Originally Zalente; however, Zaleucus was responsible for the earliest known codification of Greek Law.

[6] Originally Damazate.

[7] See introduction. Also, James Ormond led a skirmish against the O'Tooles, MacMurroughs, and the O'Mores "in the parts of Leys by Athy" in July of 1359 (Otay-Ruthven, 283).

[8] Sir Edwards Perrers @1397 temporarily replaced Roger Mortimer, fourth earl of March, seventh earl of Ulster, and appointed lieutenant of Ireland by Richard II, as March accompanied Richard in England (Otay-Ruthven 335). March was removed from office during the summer of 1397 when suspicions by Richard also extended to Gloucester, Warwick, Arundel, and the Archbishop (Otay-Ruthven 337).

[9] "Fraunchise" is the Middle English word for generosity. As Yonge continually refers to this attribute throughout the manuscript, this translation will remain consistent with all mentioning of the original word.

[10] The Middle English word, "largesse," in the 13th through 16th centuries, was interpreted as "liberality, bountifulness, or munificence" (OED).

[11] The original word used for prudence is "purveyaunce," another favorite of Yonge's. The use of this simpler word encourages the text to flow and will be used to reinforce and retain a stentorian tone (OED).

[12] The original word for shun is "enchou." Although the nearest relative word is eschew, the translated word "shun" is chosen to retain the flavor of the text.

[13] Once an associate of the Apostle Paul in Asia Minor, Hermogenes, along with Phygelus, deserted him possibly due to the constraints of discipleship (New American Bible, 2Tim 1:15-16, 1314).

[14] 1 Kings: Ch 9.

[15] Proverbs 23.

[16] This passage is reminiscent of Lollardy, which was an outgrowth of the Church of England, as well as the Catholic Church's condemnation of John Wycliffe's profession that all things depend upon the grace of God and not man, in other words, "sola gratis."

[17] Sir Stephen Scrope arrived in Ireland on August 23, 1401 and as a deputy of Richard II, became ruler of Ireland for the next few years in Thomas of Lancaster's absence. Scrope left Ireland poor and "in great desolation" and James le Butler's father, the third earl of Ormond, was made emergency governor at Scrope's departure (Otay-Ruthven 341-344).

[18] James le Butler's father, who was an appointed deputy, died in September 1405; the fifth earl of Kildare was chosen by the Irish council to succeed him. Scrope, returning to Ireland in 1407, took a tour of Ormond lands, which were in a wardship, "gaue an overthrow to the Irish of Mounster, by whome Teige O'Keruell, prince of the territory of Elye, was slain". At the end of that year, Scrope returned to England on December 8, appointed James le Butler (then around 17) as the new earl of Ormond and as deputy in Scrope's absence (Otway-Ruthven 344-345).

[19] The term "subtlety of understanding" is left as a direct translation in order to enhance the pedagogical and direct nature of the document.

[20] The original word used in the phrase, "*from* the people", is "anent". Due to the multitude of definitions regarding this Middle English standard word, the intent of the sentence must always take precedence. Therefore in this case, anent becomes the preposition, "from."

[21] In this instance, "anent" is translate as "towards" to relay direction.

[22] The word "heart" is derived from the ME "corage."

[23] Originally, "This is sayde in lyckenys."

[24] The word "meat" is used synonymously with "meal."

[25] The word " equal" is translated from the Latin "prer."

[26] According to the OED, *the Four Books*, or *the Book of the Sentence(s)*, (in Latin-the *Sententiarum libri quatuor)*, consist of a compilation of the opinions of the Church fathers on questions of Christian doctrine. Peter Lombard wrote *the Book of the Sentence(s)* in the 12th century, and he was known as the "Master of the Sentences." In addition, the "Reading of the Sentences' could mean either the office of lecturing on the 'Books of Sentences' or the special mark of the second of the three stages of the degree of Bachelor of Divinity in mediæval universities.

[27] As Yonge prefers to announce the cardinal virtues in Latin, I will follow in turn. However, in order to maintain conformity of meaning, "prudence" will be used in its modern English form throughout the text itself and as an interpretation of "purveyance.

[28] Originally "delyuernesse", deliverance is a word used to mean regularity of the bowels.

[29] Here again, "anent", is translated in another variation of meaning as "towards."

[30] The King of France is also mentioned as the Fulk of Anjou in Yonge's original footnote.

[31] In Yonge's original footnote, mind is equated with memory.

[32] An ell equals 45 inches or 112.5 centimeters.

[33] Physicians and leeches are interchangeable terms; however on occasion when both are used, both will be included.

[34] Yonge originally refers to Cicero by his middle name; Cicero's full name was Marcus Tullius Cicero. Cicero was born in 106 BC and was murdered in 43 BC; his life coincides with the fall of the Roman Empire. Cicero held politics in greater esteem than philosophy and the only times he wrote philosophic works was when he was barred from politics.

[35] This is a difficult passage as the original sentence uses "lesynge" (lying and liar) and "losyngere" (flattery); however, the author's previous usage takes precedence and the phrase is directly translated.

[36] See introduction.

[37] Yonge originally calls Matthew Paris, "Parisiensis." Paris was a Benedictine monk and chronicler (1200-1259). A noted English historian, he was known for his style, range of interest and detailed information. His greatest work was the "Chronica Majora" which records history from creation until 1259.

[38] Yonge follows precisely the story given in Kings II.

[39] Possibly Yonge confuses the name O'Dennis with O'Dempsey as the latter was present in the battle of the red moors of Athy, fighting against James le Butler's grandfather, James, Earl of Ormond, the chaste. No other record is found naming the family of O'Dennis during this time period.

[40] In early 1377, "Art, son of Dermot McMorgh" bound himself and his "nation" to Ormond and "adherence to be faithful and to go to war with the king against the Irish insurgents of Leinster with all his power, and to make faithful stay with the king for a year from February 2, receiving a fee of 40 marks" (Otway-Ruthven 310). As wars and infractions were common, the MacMurroughs would swear obeisance to both Richard II and York, however, it would be the latter that would finally hold them to peace.

[41] The following story is a traditional anecdote related through the centuries regarding the despotic Persian King, Cambyses II (? -522 BC), son of Cyrus the Great.

[42] Augustine's work, *De moribus ecclesiae catholicae et de moribus Manichaeorum* (The Customs of the Catholic Church and the Customs of the Manichees) is a general apologetic treatise comparing the two ways of life. It is generally listed as an anti-Manichean document.

[43] Although there are three Maurice Fitz Geralds in Irish history, I believe Yonge makes reference to Maurice I who died in 1176. All the latter Irish men mentioned were historic figures during the Norman conquest of Ireland.

[44] Yonge names Vegetius as "Vegesce."

[45] Substituted as rather, the original word is "leuer" from which "lief" is derived.

[46] Yonge uses the original term, "mulion," which is the Middle English word, "muleteer."

[47] Richard Cambrensis is actually Gerald Cambrensis or Gerald of Wales.

[48] According to Otway-Ruthven, Dermot's flight to England in 1166 is considered the beginning of the Norman Conquest; however, it was only at the intervention of Henry II in 1171 that the Irish situation changed. Dermot obtained strong Norman allies, including Richard fitz Gilbert de Clare, lord of Strigoil and earl of Pembroke, aka Strongbow. The latter married Dermot's daughter and later gained de Courcy as an ally.

[49] According to myth, as cited by Elizabeth Matthew, Gurgent, the son of Britain's King Belyng, was the ruler of Bayonne, the capital of the Basque country and origin of Irish settlers; through their Spanish connection, the colonists and their newly acquired land became the property of the King of England. She also notes that an early king of Ireland "paid tribute to King Arthur and various other kings of the isles" (151). However, H. R. Montgomery Hitchcock recalls a common Celtic myth that disagrees with Yonge's version: "The [Spanish] Milesians derive their name from Milesius, or Gallamh, grandson of Breógan (Bryan?), from whom the Brigantes of Spain, according to Keating, were descenced. Milesius was like Moses in this, that he never set foot upon the promised land, dying before the expedition set forth to avenge the death of his uncle, Ith. Hoewer, his widow, Scota, an Egyptian princess, and his eight sons, Donn, Ir, Aireach, Feabhruadh, Arranan, Colpa, Heber, Heremon, and Amergin took part in the invasion, which the uncles of Milesius organized. That expedition was disastrous to many of them, for Scota perished with five of her sons, and the country was eventually divided between Heber and Heremon" (15).

[50] Originally "at the Isle of Orcades;" Also known as the "Outer Islands," it is unknown at which of the twenty Scottish islands located north of the mainland city of Wick in the Scottish Highlands that this meeting supposedly occurred. Also, Yonge's imperialistic intentions betray him, as the only resistance the Spanish Milesians actually encountered in obtaining new Irish territory was a storm at sea (MacManus 10).

[51] According to the legend, the Milesians, Eber and Eremon, divided the land between themselves. Eremon received the northern half of Ireland and Eber, the southern (Seumas MacManus 11).

[52] The original word Yonge uses for district is "candrede." According to the OED, a candrede is defined as one hundred and it has been used since 1387 to signify "a district containing one hundred townships."

[53] According to the OED, a weapontaille is another spelling of "wapentake." The definition used since 1000AD is one of a subdivision of certain English shires according to the "hundred" of other counties. A "hundred" is a subdivision of a county or shire, having its own court; a "hundred" was also formerly applied to the court itself.

[54] Yonge errs; the actual date is October 1171.

[55] Dermot is also known at this point as Dermot MacCarthy of Desmond (Otway-Ruthven 49).

[56] Dunvenald is also known as Donald O'Brien (Otway-Ruthven 49).

[57] Offelan is located within the central part of County Kildare.

[58] Yonge cites three cases, but adds another.

[59] Derived from the Anglo-Saxon word "loece," which means to heal, medieval doctors were called leeches. The leech was used for bloodletting in their patients, which was considered

necessary to cure many illnesses. Common areas of the body that leeches were attached to were areas such as the gums, lips, nose, and fingers, and in some cases, even the pubic area.

[60] Yonge originally uses "Nenuve" and also "Nynyvee" in the following chapter.

[61] See introduction.

[62] According to Otway-Ruthven, this incident occurred in May of 1421 (360). Matthew suggests that Yonge, "in his concern to prove the efficacy of prayer, compressed events (i.e. three months time)" (140). Also, it is interesting to note that despite the grand deeds of le Butler, immediately after his commission expired, his conquests became the conquerors. Ormond stressed Anglo-Norman rule of the Irish; however the Irish had other ideas.

[63] The passage within parenthesis is actually a gloss and not a literal translation.

[64] In the original document, Yonge mistakenly says, "Taste is a common sense spread..." instead of touch.

[65] The original word used here is "tokenesse;" "signs" will henceforth be used in all places that use the word, "tokens" in order to clarify meaning.

[66] Yonge was a notary, which leads one to wonder how much of this paragraph is of his own design.

[67] The book is also known as *Kapirhc* and is simply a collection of aphorisms.

[68] "Philemon" in the Latin; according to Steele, he can be identified with Polemon, an early writer on the science of physiognomy (Lydgate and Burgh's Secrees, viii).

[69] "Complexcioun" is used to signify temperament.

[70] Yonge originally uses "parcenere" and "partifelewe" as partaker and sharer. It is unclear, what, if any distinction is being made. Middle (and Renaissance) English prose favored the rhetorical style of "doubling" (placing two synonyms side by side).

[71] Yonge uses the word, "harde", to define coarse hair. The original term can also mean firm, harsh, obdurate, difficult and stiff.

[72] Yonge uses "curlyours" to signify a type of bird, however, Steele translates this word as "Curlew." The OED defines the noun as an obs. form of quail. I have used "pins" as a translation for "pennes." Birds have different types of feathers, pins being one kind.

[73] Throughout the text, "heart" and "courage" are used interchangeably. The decision to use either of the two is dictated by the intent of the sentence within which it is found.

[74] Originally, "a dredful or a feynte man."

[75] Yonge oddly uses "vp-rerid" to signify the "upper" lip; in earlier cases up-reared simply means up-raised.

[76] In the Middle Ages, an electuary was a medicinal paste consisting of powder mixed with honey, or some sort of syrup, in order to preserve it.

[77] The title, "Summer," as well as "Autumn" and "Winter" in the following two chapters, were not included in either of the original manuscripts. These headings were inserted by Robert Steele to signify a natural section/change of topic within the text.

[78] Agarik, a fungus, was noted for its use as a cathartic

142

Works Cited

Bliss, Alan, and Joseph Long. "Literature in Norman French and English." A New History of Ireland. Ed. Art Cosgrove. Vol. 2. Oxford: Clarendon, 1987. 708-736.

Chaucer, Geoffrey. The Riverside Chaucer. Ed. F. N. Robinson. 3rd ed. Boston: Houghton, 1987.

Cosgrove, Art. "The Emergence of the Pale, 1399-1447." Ed. Art Cosgrove. Vol 2. A New History of Ireland. Oxford: Clarendon, 1987. 353-556.

Curtis, Edmund. A History Medieval Ireland. New York: Barnes & Noble, 1968.

Deane, Seamus. The Field Day Anthology of Irish Writing. 1. Derry: Field Day Publications, 1991.

Dolan, T. P. "James Yonge." Eds. H. C. G. Matthew and Brian Harrison. Oxford Dictionary of National Biography. 60. Oxford: Oxford UP, 2004. 811-812.

Dolan, Terrence. "Writing in Ireland." Ed. David Wallace. The Cambridge History of Medieval English Literature. Cambridge: Cambridge UP, 1999. 208-228.

Hitchcock, F. R. Montgomery. The Midland Septs and the Pale. Bowie: Heritage, 1998.

Irish Historical Documents 1172-1922. Ed. and trans. E. Curtis and R. B. McDowell. London: Methuen, 1943.

Kingsford, C. L. First English Life of Henry V. Ed. C. L. Kingsford. Oxford: Clarendon Press, 1911.

Lydgate, John, and Benedict Burgh. Foreword. Secrees of Old Philisoffres. Ed. Robert Steele. London: Kegan Paul, Trench, Trübner & Co., 1894. vii-xxi.

MacManus, Seumas. The Story of the Irish Race. New York: Wings Books, 1990.

Manzalaoui, M. A. "Philip of Tripoli and His Textual Methods." Eds. W.F. Ryan & Charles B. Schmitt. Pseudo-Aristotle: The Secrets of Secrets. London: Warburg Institute, 1982.

---. Introduction. Secretum Secretorum: Nine English Versions. Ed. M. A. Manzalaoui. Oxford: Oxford UP, 1977.

Matthew, E. A. E. "Butler, James, fourth earl of Ormond (1390-1452)." Eds. H. C. G. Matthew and Brian Harrison. Oxford Dictionary of National Biography. Vol. 9. Oxford: Oxford UP, 2004. 147-149.

---. "The Governing of the Lancastrian Lordship of Ireland in the Time of James Butler, Fourth Earl of Ormond, c. 1420-1452." PhD. Diss. University of Durham, 1994.

Otway-Ruthven, A. J. A History of Medieval Ireland. New York: Barnes &Noble, 1968.

Oxford English Dictionary. Ed. J.A. Simpson and E.S.C. Weiner. 2nd ed. Oxford: Clarendon Press, 1989. OED Online Oxford University Press. 4 Apr. 2000. http://exlibris.lib.memphis.edu: 2083.

Pearsall, Derek. "Hoccleve's Regement of Princes: The Poetics of Royal Self Representation." Speculum 69.2 (1994). 386-410.

144

Pseudo-Aristotle. The Gouernaunce of Prynces. Trans. James Yonge. Ed. Robert Steele. London: Kegan Paul, Trench, Trübner & Co., 1898. 121-250.

Seymour, St. John D. Anglo-Irish Literature 1200-1582. Cambridge: Cambridge UP, 1929.

Simms, Katharine. "The Norman Invasion and the Gaelic Recovery." The Oxford Illustrated History of Ireland. Ed. R.F. Foster. Oxford: Oxford University Press, 1989. 53–103.

Stanford, W. B. Ireland and the Classical Tradition. Totowa: Rowman & Littlefield, 1977.

Watt, J. A. "The Anglo-Irish colony under strain, 1327-99." Ed. Art Cosgrove. Vol. 2 A New History of Ireland. Oxford: Clarendon, 1987. 352-396.

Williams, Stephen J. The Secret of Secrets. Ann Arbor: U of MI P, 2003.

Wylie, J. H., and W. T. Waugh. The Reign of Henry V. 3. Cambridge: Cambridge UP, 1929.

Suggested Reading List

Corish, Patrick J. A History of Irish Catholicism. Dublin: Gill, 1967.

Canny, Nicholas. The Oxford History of Ireland. Ed. R. F. Foster. Oxford: Oxford UP, 1992. 88-133.

Dolley, Michael. Anglo-Norman Ireland. Dublin: Gill and MacMillan Ltd., 1972.

Duffy, Seán, Ireland in the Middle Ages. Basingstoke: Macmillan Press, 1997.

Frame, Robin. "Les Engleys Neés en Irlande: The English Political Identity in Medieval Ireland." Transactions of the Royal Historical Society. 6 (1993): 83–103; also in Frame, Robin, Ireland and Britain 1170–1450. London: Hambledon Press, 1998. 131–50.

Furnivall, Frederick James. The English conquest of Ireland, A.D. 1166-1185. New York,: Greenwood Press, 1969.

Kerby-Fulton, Kathryn, and Despres, Denise L. "Iconography and the Professional Reader: the Politics of Book Production in the Douce Piers Plowman." Medieval Cultures. 15. Minneapolis: University of Minnesota Press, 1999.

Kerby-Fulton, Kathryn, and Justice, Steven. "Langlandian Reading Circles and the Civil Service in London and Dublin, 1380–1427." New Medieval Literatures. I. Eds. Wendy Scase, Rita Copeland and David Lawton. Oxford: Clarendon Press, 1997. 59–83.

Lydon, James. Ireland in the Later Middle Ages. Dublin: Gill and MacMillan Ltd., 1973.

Lydon, James. "The Middle Nation." The English in Medieval Ireland. Ed. James Lydon. Dublin: Royal Irish Academy, 1984. 1–26.

Lydon, James. "Nation and Race in Medieval Ireland." Concepts of National Identity in the Middle Ages. Ed. S. Forde, L. Johnson and A.V. Murray Leeds, 1995, 103–124.

Lydon, J. F. The Lordship of Ireland in the Middle Ages. Dublin: Gill and MacMillan Ltd., 1972.

Scott, K. "A Mid-Fifteenth-Century English Illuminating Shop and its Customers." Journal of the Warburg and Courtauld Institutes. 31. 1968. 170–96.

The Course of Irish History. Rev. ed. Eds. T. W. Moody and F. X. Martin. Lanham: Roberts Rinehart Publishers, 1994.

The Oxford Companion to Irish History. 2nd Ed. Ed. S. J. Connolly. Oxford: Oxford UP. 2004.